meijer ®

BASIC CAR CARE

From Haynes Manuals - the World's Authority on Car Repair

Contents

ABOUT THIS GUIDE

This Basic Car Care Guide was written to provide general information on a variety of automotive topics of interest to the do-it-yourselfer. Although helpful, this guide cannot possibly provide comprehensive information for the numerous makes and models of vehicles on the road today. It is highly recommended that you invest in a repair manual written specifically for your vehicle. This manual will give easy-to-follow instructions for basic maintenance jobs (like those shown in this Guide), as well as more involved repair procedures. It will be illustrated with step-by-step photos and drawings showing exactly the same components on your car or truck. These manuals are commonly available at your local auto parts store.

© **Haynes North America, Inc. 2005**
With permission from J.H. Haynes & Co. Ltd.

Printed in the U.S.A.

ISBN 1 56392 572 9

Library of Congress Control Number 2005921150

General information you should know

GENERAL INFORMATION YOU SHOULD KNOW

My Vehicle Form

Make: _____

Model:_____

Year:_____

Body style: _____

Vehicle Identification Number (VIN):_____

License plate number:_____ Expiration month: _____

Engine

    Type:_____

    Displacement:_____

    Number of cylinders:_____

Air filter:_____

Fuel filter:_____

Engine oil

    Type: _____

    Capacity (with filter): _____

    Filter type: _____

Cooling system

    Capacity: _____

    Coolant type: _____

Power steering fluid type: _____

Battery

    Group size: _____ CCA (Cold Cranking Amp) rating:_____

Spark plug

    Type:_____ Gap: _____

Transmission

Manual   Automatic

    Lubricant type: _____   Fluid type:_____

    Capacity: _____   Capacity: _____

Tires

    Type: _____ Size: _____

Front/Rear air pressure: _____/_____

Vehicle Identification Number (VIN) guide

The Vehicle Identification Number, or VIN number, as it's usually called, is a long string of numbers and letters imprinted on a small plate located on the driver's side of the dashboard. Most people know that these numbers are the means by which a vehicle is identified by the state in which the vehicle is licensed and registered. But what most people don't know is that those numbers mean a lot more than simply the "number" of a vehicle. Once you know what each individual number or letter represents, you can learn all sorts of information about your vehicle. We'll only deal with the two most important characters of the VIN - the model year code and the engine code (which will reveal the number of cylinders, displacement and in some cases, the type of fuel system). There may be occasions when you'll have refer to the VIN number when you're buying parts for your vehicle. It's a good idea to record your VIN on the "My Vehicle Form" near the front of this manual for reference.

Engine code

Since 1981, the engine code is usually the eighth character in the VIN on most North American cars and trucks. On many imports, however, the engine code may be the fourth, fifth or sixth character. This code may be required when purchasing certain parts for your vehicle.

Model year code

On almost all vehicles produced since 1981, the model year code is the tenth character of the VIN. The same model year codes are used by all manufacturers:

B = 1981	N = 1992
C = 1982	P = 1993
D = 1983	R = 1994
E = 1984	S = 1995
F = 1985	T = 1996
G = 1986	V = 1997
H = 1987	W = 1998
J = 1988	X = 1999
K = 1989	Y = 2000
L = 1990	1 = 2001
M = 1991	2 = 2002

MAINTENANCE SCHEDULE

Every 250 miles or once a week, whichever comes first
Check the engine oil level
Check the engine coolant level
Check the windshield washer fluid level
Check the brake and the clutch fluid level
Check the tires and tire pressures

Every 3000 miles or 3 months, whichever comes first
All items listed above, plus:
Check the power steering fluid level
Check the automatic transmission/transaxle fluid level
Change the engine oil and oil filter
Lubricate the chassis (if equipped with grease fittings)

Every 6000 miles or 6 months, whichever comes first
All items listed above, plus:
Check and service the battery
Inspect and replace, if necessary, the windshield wiper blades
Rotate the tires
Inspect the exhaust system
Check the seat belt operation

Every 15,000 miles or 12 months, whichever comes first
All items listed above, plus:
Inspect and replace, if necessary, all underhood hoses
Inspect the cooling system
Check the fuel system
Replace the fuel filter
Inspect the steering and suspension components
Inspect the brakes
Check the manual transmission/transaxle lubricant level
Check the transfer case lubricant level (four-wheel drive vehicles)
Check the rear axle (differential) lubricant level (four-wheel and
    rear-wheel drive vehicles)
Check the front (differential) lubricant level (four-wheel drive vehicles)
Replace the interior ventilation filter (if equipped)

Every 30,000 miles or 24 months, whichever comes first
Replace the filter element in the air cleaner
Service the cooling system (drain, flush and refill)
Change the automatic transmission/transaxle fluid and filter
Inspect the wheel bearings
Change the brake fluid
Replace the spark plugs

Every 50,000 miles or 48 months, whichever comes first
Check the engine drivebelt(s)
Inspect and replace, if necessary, the spark plug wires
Change the manual transmission/transaxle lubricant
Change the transfer case lubricant (four-wheel drive vehicles)
Change the rear axle (differential) lubricant (four-wheel and
    rear-wheel drive vehicles)

Date Mileage	Work performed	Parts/supplies Comments	Cost

TIRE SIZE MARKINGS

All tires carry standard tire size markings on their sidewalls, such as "**195/60 R 15 87H**".

195 indicates the width of the tire in mm.

60 indicates the ratio of the tire section height to width, expressed as a percentage. If no number is present at this point, the ratio is considered to be 82%.

R indicates the tire is of radial ply construction.

15 indicates the wheel diameter for the tire is 15 inches.

87 is an index number which indicates the maximum load that the tire can carry at maximum speed.

H represents the maximum speed for the tire which should be equal to or greater than the car's maximum speed.

Note that some tires have the speed rating symbol located between the tire width and the wheel diameter, attached to the "R" radial tire reference, for example, "195/60 HR 15".

SPEED RATING SYMBOLS FOR RADIAL TIRES

Symbol	mph
P	93
Q	99
R	106
S	112
T	118
U	124
V (after size markings)	Up to 150
H (within size markings)	Up to 130
V (within size markings)	Over 130
Z (within size markings)	Over 150

Booster battery (jump) starting

Observe these precautions when using a booster battery to start a vehicle:

a) *Before connecting the booster battery, make sure the ignition switch is in the OFF position.*

b) *Turn off the lights, heater and other electrical loads.*

c) *Your eyes should be shielded. Safety goggles are a good idea.*

d) *Make sure the booster battery is the same voltage as the dead one in the vehicle.*

e) *The two vehicles MUST NOT TOUCH each other!*

f) *Make sure the transaxle is in Neutral (manual) or Park (automatic).*

g) *If the booster battery is not a maintenance-free type, remove the vent caps and lay a cloth over the vent holes.*

h) *On some vehicles the battery is remotely mounted, such as in the trunk or behind a front fender, forward of the wheelwell.*

Depending on the location of the battery, in some cases, remote battery connections are provided inside the engine compartment for jump-starting and easy battery disconnection.

Connect the red colored jumper cable to the positive (+) terminal of booster battery and the other end to the positive (+) terminal of the battery or to the positive remote terminal inside the engine compartment. Then connect one end of the black colored jumper cable to the negative (-) terminal of the booster battery and other end of the cable to a good ground point on the engine of the disabled vehicle or to the negative (-) remote terminal.

Start the engine using the booster battery then, with the engine running at idle speed disconnect the jumper cables in the reverse order of connection.

On vehicles with a remotely mounted battery, the remote battery terminals are located in the engine compartment and are well marked - when connecting jumper cables connect the cable to the positive terminal (A) first, then the negative terminal (B)

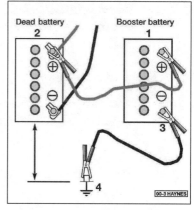

Make the booster cable connections in the numerical order shown (note that the negative cable of the booster battery is NOT attached to the negative terminal of the dead battery)

Do's and Don'ts to keep your engine in tip-top condition

DO check the engine oil level every week, and before a long trip.

DO change the engine oil and filter every 3,000 miles or six months.

DO check the coolant level and the drivebelt(s) regularly.

DO take the car out for a long trip occasionally, if you normally only use it for short trips.

DO stop immediately if the oil pressure warning light comes on when you're driving - it's not an oil level warning light, and you'll wreck the engine if you don't stop very quickly!

DON'T warm the engine up by leaving the car parked with the engine running - it's better just to start the engine and drive off, even in winter.

DON'T warm the engine up by revving it more than normal.

DON'T rev the engine more than you need to until the temperature gauge has reached its normal position.

DON'T keep driving the car if you know the engine is overheating.

Getting ready for winter

What to check before winter starts

CHECK THE COOLANT MIXTURE

If the coolant (antifreeze and water) freezes, it could wreck your engine. A repair shop can check the coolant for you, or you can buy a simple and inexpensive coolant tester. Except in an emergency, never fill your cooling system with plain water, even in summer - antifreeze stops corrosion inside the engine as well as protecting against the cold.

CHECK THE BATTERY

Battery failure is the most common source of trouble in winter. Check that the battery is in good condition, then clean the battery cable connections, and make sure they're tight. If the battery shows signs that it might be getting towards the end of its life, install a new one before winter starts.

CHECK THE WIPERS AND WASHERS

You'll use them a lot more in winter. Make sure the wiper blades are in good condition (new ones aren't expensive, so it's well worth replacing them at the start of every winter anyway). Check the windshield (and tailgate, if you have one) washer system.

CHECK THE COOLING SYSTEM HOSES

Look for signs of damage or leaks, and have any problem hoses replaced.

CHECK THE DRIVEBELT(S)

Look for damage, and check the tension of the belt(s).

CHECK ALL FLUIDS AND FILTERS

Add or replace if necessary.

CHECK ALL THE LIGHTS AND INDICATORS

Make sure that they work properly, and replace any blown bulbs.

Tools

It's wise to carry a small set of basic tools in a box or container in the trunk in case of problems or a minor emergency on the road.

WORK GLOVES

Your hands can get pretty dirty even changing a tire and at times like that it's nice to have a pair of inexpensive work gloves in the trunk. Gloves can also prevent burns and cuts if you have to work on a hot engine in the engine compartment or under the vehicle.

LOCKING PLIERS

This versatile tool can be used as pliers, an adjustable wrench or as a clamp. A pair of needle-nose pliers is also very useful.

SCREWDRIVER SET

A small selection of flat blade and Phillips head screwdrivers doesn't take up much room can be very useful for emergency repairs.

CRESCENT WRENCH

A crescent wrench can be adjusted to fit a range of nuts and bolts.

DUCT TAPE

A roll of professional-grade duct tape of the type used by air conditioning contractors can be useful for many types of emergency repairs. The tape should be marked "200°" or "250°" which means you can use it to repair a radiator or heater hose in a pinch.

TIRE PRESSURE GAUGE

Gas station air hoses (when you can find one that works) have notoriously inaccurate air gauges. Having your own pressure gauge allows you to detect under-inflated tires or a slow leak that could prove disastrous at freeway speeds.

RAGS OR A ROLL OF PAPER TOWELS

If anything can go wrong it will. If that involves a spill, a leak or windows that need cleaning, there is no substitute for clean rags or paper towels.

Warranties, recalls and TSB's
Warranties

A new vehicle warranty typically lasts 3 years or 36,000 miles, whichever comes first. In recent years government-mandated warranties on most components in the emissions and fuel system have been extended to as long as 8 years or 80,000 miles, whichever comes first, depending on which laws apply. These components can include virtually the complete fuel system up to and including the tank itself.

Other parts of the vehicle such as the safety restraint system (airbags and seat belts) and body rust-through protection are usually warranted for a longer period (usually around 5 years). The tire warranty is between the owner and the tire manufacturer.

Since geographic differences sometimes apply, it's best to consult your warranty booklet to determine just what parts are covered in your area.

Recalls

Recalls are repairs suggested by automobile manufacturers and the U.S. National Highway Traffic Safety Administration (NHTSA) to ensure the safety or mechanical integrity of your car. These repairs are necessary due to a factory defect or oversight, and, as such, they are done free of charge by any new-car dealership authorized to sell your type of car. You can check whether a recall exists for your car by calling NHTSA at 1-800-424-9393. If there is a recall involving your particular vehicle, have it serviced as soon as possible, since many recalls involve serious safety issues.

Technical Service Bulletins (TSB's)

Every year the car manufacturers issue hundreds of TSB's to the service departments of new-car dealerships. TSB's provide the dealership mechanics with information about specific, common problems with particular cars and the best methods to fix them. TSB's, by law, must be made available for review by the vehicle owner upon request. Although dealership service departments aren't always cooperative in this way, independent repair shops often have access to TSB's through their reference sources. When your vehicle has a problem, ask whether there's a TSB concerning it, which will remind the mechanic to do his research!

How a car works

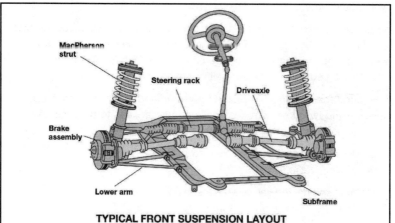

MacPherson strut

Steering rack

Driveaxle

Brake assembly

Lower arm

Subframe

TYPICAL FRONT SUSPENSION LAYOUT

BCC-1-HAYNES

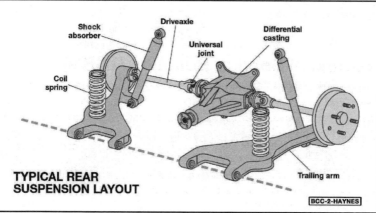

Shock absorber

Driveaxle

Differential casting

Universal joint

Coil spring

TYPICAL REAR SUSPENSION LAYOUT

Trailing arm

BCC-2-HAYNES

The Engine

How does it work?

The engine is a machine which converts chemical energy (hydrocarbons in the fuel) into mechanical energy in the form of motion. It does this by burning fuel inside its cylinders - hence the term "internal combustion engine."

Fuel/air mixture is drawn into a cylinder, and the mixture is compressed by a piston and burned. When the mixture burns, it expands very quickly and pushes the piston down the cylinder.

The piston is connected to the crankshaft by a connecting rod which rotates the crankshaft. The crankshaft is connected to the transmission, which drives the car's wheels.

Intake and exhaust valves at the top of the cylinder allow the fuel/air mixture into the cylinder, and burned gases out into the exhaust system. The valves are opened and closed by a camshaft, which is driven from the crankshaft, usually by a timing belt or timing chain.

In a four-stroke engine, the piston moves up and down twice (two up-strokes, and two down-strokes, making four strokes), to produce one pulse of power. The four strokes are:

a) *Intake* - *the piston moves down, sucking fuel/air mixture into the cylinder via the intake valve.*

b) *Compression* - *the valves are closed and the piston moves up, compressing the mixture until it's ignited at the top of the stroke.*

c) *Power* - *the piston is pushed down as the burning mixture expands.*

d) *Exhaust* - *the piston moves back up the cylinder (due to the momentum produced during the power stroke), and the burned gases are pushed out through the open exhaust valve. The cycle then starts again, with another intake stroke.*

On gasoline engines the fuel/air mixture is ignited by a spark from the spark plug.

On diesel engines the intake valve lets air into the cylinder; the fuel is injected straight into the cylinder by a fuel injector (fuel is pumped to the injector by a fuel injection pump). When the fuel/air mixture is compressed, the temperature rises very quickly, and the mixture ignites by itself.

Multi-valve engines

Most older car engines have one intake valve and one exhaust valve per cylinder - i.e., two valves per cylinder. Many modern engines have three, four, or in a few cases even five valves per cylinder, although the most common configuration is four valves per cylinder. Such an engine has two intake valves and two exhaust valves for each cylinder (so a four-cylinder engine would be a "16-valve" engine).

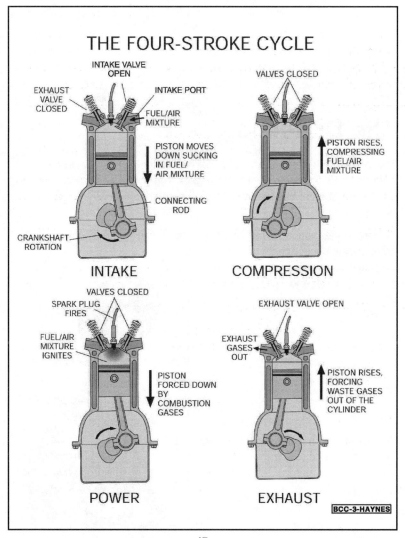

THE FOUR-STROKE CYCLE

INTAKE
- INTAKE VALVE OPEN
- EXHAUST VALVE CLOSED
- INTAKE PORT
- FUEL/AIR MIXTURE
- PISTON MOVES DOWN SUCKING IN FUEL/AIR MIXTURE
- CONNECTING ROD
- CRANKSHAFT ROTATION

COMPRESSION
- VALVES CLOSED
- PISTON RISES, COMPRESSING FUEL/AIR MIXTURE

POWER
- VALVES CLOSED
- SPARK PLUG FIRES
- FUEL/AIR MIXTURE IGNITES
- PISTON FORCED DOWN BY COMBUSTION GASES

EXHAUST
- EXHAUST VALVE OPEN
- EXHAUST GASES OUT
- PISTON RISES, FORCING WASTE GASES OUT OF THE CYLINDER

BCC-3-HAYNES

Using multiple valves gives improved efficiency, because they allow the fuel/air mixture to enter the cylinder, and the exhaust gases to leave, more easily.

Double-overhead-camshaft engines

Double-overhead-camshaft (or "twin-cam") engines have two camshafts, one operating the exhaust valves, and one operating the intake valves. Multi-valve engines are almost always double-overhead-camshaft engines.

The Driveline

The driveline is a term for the group of components which transmits power from the car's engine to the driven wheels. The components used depend on whether the car has the front wheels, rear wheels, or all four wheels driven.

As well as the manual transmission or automatic transmission, the other components used include a clutch (manual transmission only), a differential, driveaxle, and, on rear-wheel-drive and four-wheel-drive cars, a driveshaft.

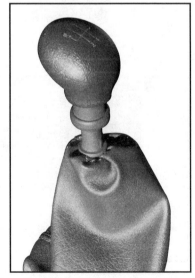

HOW A CAR WORKS

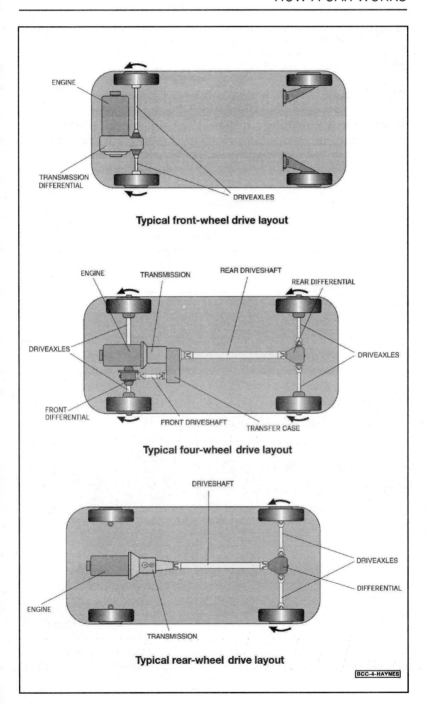

Typical front-wheel drive layout

Typical four-wheel drive layout

Typical rear-wheel drive layout

BCC-4-HAYNES

19

The Cooling system
Keeping the engine cool

On all modern cars, the cooling system is pressurized, and consists of a radiator (mounted at the front of the engine compartment), a coolant (water) pump (mounted on the engine), a cooling fan (which cools the radiator), a thermostat, and an expansion tank.

The radiator usually has two narrow tanks, joined by a honeycombed metal matrix (sometimes called a core). The coolant (a mixture of water and antifreeze) flows from one tank, through the matrix to the other tank. On some cars with automatic transmission, a transmission fluid cooler is built into the radiator. The radiator relies on the flow of air through the

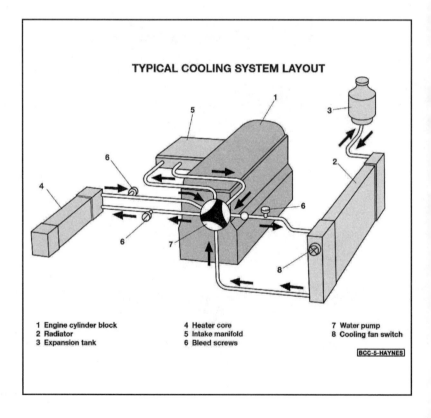

TYPICAL COOLING SYSTEM LAYOUT

1 Engine cylinder block	4 Heater core	7 Water pump
2 Radiator	5 Intake manifold	8 Cooling fan switch
3 Expansion tank	6 Bleed screws	

BCC-5-HAYNES

matrix produced by the car's forward motion, supplemented by the cooling fan when necessary, to cool the coolant inside.

The water pump is driven by the engine's timing belt or chain, or by an auxiliary drivebelt. Most water pumps consist of a rotating impeller inside a housing.

The cooling fan draws cool air over the radiator when the speed of the car is too low, or the air temperature is too high, to give enough cooling. The cooling fan is usually electrically-operated, although some older cars may have a belt-driven fan. A few cars have a viscous fan attached to one of the engine pulleys - a viscous fluid coupling causes the fan to turn as the engine heats up.

The thermostat is normally located inside a housing on the engine. Its job is to allow the engine to warm up quickly by restricting the flow of coolant to the radiator when cold, and also to regulate the normal operating temperature of the engine.

The system uses a pressure cap, either on the expansion tank or on the radiator. The pressure cap effectively pressurizes the cooling system as the temperature rises, which raises the boiling point of the coolant. It acts as a safety valve by venting steam or hot coolant if the pressure rises above a certain level. The pressure cap also acts as a vacuum relief valve to stop a vacuum forming in the system as it cools.

The expansion tank allows room for the coolant to expand as it heats up. Any air or gas bubbles which form in the coolant return to the expansion tank, and are released in the air space above the coolant.

Ignition and fuel systems

The ignition system creates the sparks which are used to ignite the fuel/air mixture on a gasoline engine (diesel engines don't have an ignition system). The ignition coil uses low-voltage electricity from the battery to produce the high-voltage electricity which is sent along the spark plug wires (if used) to the spark plugs. The spark plugs produce sparks inside the cylinders.

The fuel system controls the amount of fuel and air burned by the engine.

Gasoline engines

Air passes through the air filter into the intake manifold, where it is mixed with fuel, before passing through the intake valves into the engine cylinders.

On older engines, a carburetor is used to mix the fuel and air. A carburetor uses the flow of air to suck fuel into the engine. It doesn't give enough control over the fuel/air mixture to enable an engine to meet modern emissions regulations.

A fuel injection system is much more efficient than a carburetor, and allows fine control of the fuel/air mixture. On a single-point fuel injection system, a fuel injector is used to spray fuel into the intake manifold, where it is mixed with air before passing to the cylinders. On a multi-point fuel injection system, one fuel injector is used for each cylinder in the engine.

Diesel engines

The air passes through the air filter into the intake manifold, and into the engine cylinders. A fuel injection pump pumps fuel to a fuel injector for each cylinder.

On an indirect injection diesel engine, the fuel injector pumps the fuel into a swirl chamber mounted in the cylinder head above the cylinder, which swirls the fuel around to mix it with the air in the cylinder. On a direct injection diesel engine, the fuel injector pumps the fuel directly into the cylinder, where it is mixed with the air.

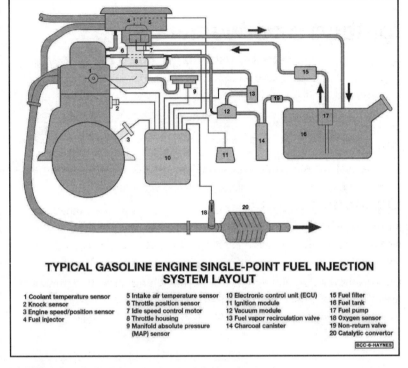

**TYPICAL GASOLINE ENGINE SINGLE-POINT FUEL INJECTION
SYSTEM LAYOUT**

1 Coolant temperature sensor	5 Intake air temperature sensor	10 Electronic control unit (ECU)	15 Fuel filter
2 Knock sensor	6 Throttle position sensor	11 Ignition module	16 Fuel tank
3 Engine speed/position sensor	7 Idle speed control motor	12 Vacuum module	17 Fuel pump
4 Fuel injector	8 Throttle housing	13 Fuel vapor recirculation valve	18 Oxygen sensor
	9 Manifold absolute pressure (MAP) sensor	14 Charcoal canister	19 Non-return valve
			20 Catalytic convertor

BCC-6-HAYNES

What to check

Air filters, fuel filters, and (on gasoline engines) the spark plugs, should all be replaced at the recommended intervals. Always make sure that the correct types of filter and spark plugs are used.

Modern fuel and ignition systems are very reliable, and most problems are due to damp, or to poor or dirty electrical connections.

• Always make sure that you have plenty of fuel in the tank - if you run out of fuel, dirt may be drawn into the fuel system from the fuel tank.

• Always replace the components at the manufacturer's recommended intervals.

• Regularly check all electrical connections and wiring.

• On diesel engines, drain water from the fuel filter regularly.

• Spray damp electrical connections with a water dispersant, such as WD-40.

• Regularly check the fuel line connections under the hood for leaks - fuel leaks are dangerous as well as expensive.

Catalytic converters

Catalytic converters are used to cut down the amount of harmful exhaust gases released into the atmosphere through the car's exhaust.

A catalyst is a substance which speeds up a chemical change, without being altered itself. The catalytic converter is a steel canister containing a ceramic honeycomb material coated with catalyst. The exhaust gases pass freely over the honeycomb, where the catalyst speeds up the change of the harmful gases into harmless gases and water vapor.

To avoid damaging the catalyst, the engine must be properly tuned, and certain gasoline additives (mainly those containing lead) should not be used.

On early vehicles with a catalytic converter, the converter works independently, and it relies on a well-maintained engine to be effective. This type of catalytic converter system is called "open-loop".

On modern vehicles, an oxygen (or "Lambda") sensor is installed in the

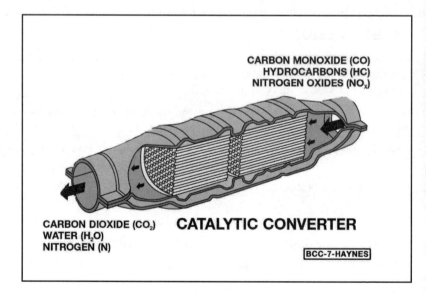

CARBON MONOXIDE (CO)
HYDROCARBONS (HC)
NITROGEN OXIDES (NO_x)

CARBON DIOXIDE (CO_2)
WATER (H_2O)
NITROGEN (N)   **CATALYTIC CONVERTER**

BCC-7-HAYNES

exhaust system. This is used by the engine management system to control the fuel/air mixture. If the mixture is kept within certain limits, the catalytic converter can work at its maximum efficiency. The Oxygen sensor sends the engine management system details of how much oxygen is in the exhaust gas, and this is used to automatically control the fuel/air mixture. This type of catalytic converter system is called "closed-loop".

After a number of years, the catalytic converter will have to be replaced, because the catalyst inside will deteriorate with age. This can be expensive because of the precious metals used to make the catalyst.

Catalytic converters have certain side-effects. First, they only work properly once they heat up to an optimum working temperature, and when they're cold, they hardly reduce pollution at all. If you're following a car with a catalytic converter, you might notice a strong "rotten egg" smell when the car accelerates hard, or when it's under a heavy load climbing a hill - this is due to hydrogen sulfide gas. Another side effect is that cars with a catalytic converter tend to produce more water from the exhaust, especially when the engine's cold, or on a short run - this means that the exhaust system tends to rust more quickly.

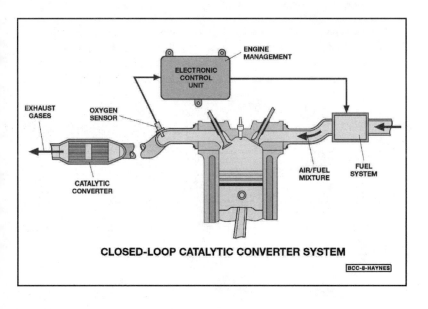

CLOSED-LOOP CATALYTIC CONVERTER SYSTEM

Engine management (computer) systems

A modern engine with an engine management system gives greater reliability, better fuel economy, better performance, and needs less maintenance than a similar older engine without engine management.

How do they work?

Various sensors monitor the engine. Each sensor produces an electrical signal, and the signal changes as the condition being monitored changes. The electrical signals are sent to an electronic control unit, which contains a microprocessor and a memory. The microprocessor processes all the information from the sensors and, by referring to its memory, can tell exactly what conditions the engine is running under. The control unit is able to "look up" values stored in its memory, and decide how much fuel the engine needs, and what the ignition timing (gasoline engines) or injection timing (diesel engines) should be at that particular instant. The control unit also controls the engine idle speed and the emission control systems.

On-board diagnostics

Engine management systems usually have an on-board diagnostic system (or self-diagnostic system) which is used to store details of any problems. If a component is faulty, the system stores a trouble code in the control unit. The trouble code can be read using a trouble code reader, or sometimes a diagnostic light on the dash, to indicate which component is faulty. This allows problems to be traced quickly and easily. For more information about On-board diagnostics, obtain a repair manual for your particular vehicle at your local auto parts store.

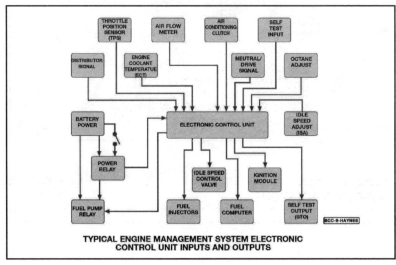

TYPICAL ENGINE MANAGEMENT SYSTEM ELECTRONIC CONTROL UNIT INPUTS AND OUTPUTS

Suspension

The suspension serves two basic purposes; it keeps the tires in contact with the road, enabling the driver to control the car, and it cushions the car's occupants from bumps and pot-holes in the road.

The design of the suspension is always a compromise, because the characteristics needed to give a comfortable ride generally won't give good handling, and vise versa. For a comfortable ride, a reasonably soft suspension is needed to cushion the body from imperfections in the road surface. For good handling, a stiff suspension is needed to keep all four tires in contact with the road, and to keep the body as still as possible.

Many older cars had independent front suspension, and a solid rear axle, while most modern cars have independent suspension front and rear. On cars with a solid rear axle, when the rear wheel on one side of the car moves, it directly affects the other rear wheel.

The suspension on most conventional cars uses a combination of springs and shock absorbers to help absorb road shocks. An anti-roll (sway) bar may be used to resist the tendency of the body to "roll" when cornering. The suspension components are mounted on the body using rubber bushings to reduce the transmission of shocks, noise and vibration from the suspension to the body.

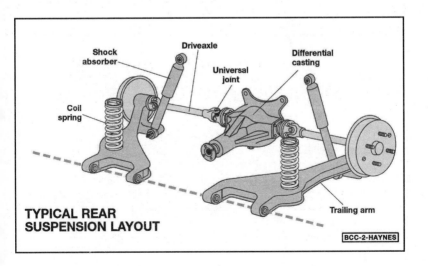

Shock absorber
Driveaxle
Differential casting
Universal joint
Coil spring
TYPICAL REAR SUSPENSION LAYOUT
Trailing arm

BCC-2-HAYNES

27

HOW A CAR WORKS

Suspension systems are very carefully and precisely designed, and the springs and shock absorbers are carefully chosen according to the weight and handling characteristics of the particular model of car.

Worn or damaged suspension components will affect the handling and braking of the car, and can be very dangerous.

Suspension problems

If the suspension components are worn or damaged, you'll probably notice that the handling and ride will suffer, and you may notice noises and rattles, especially when driving over bumps. Worn suspension components can also cause increased tire wear, and poor braking.

The suspension components are very accurately aligned, and even a small curb impact can knock out the alignment and cause tire wear. Many tire specialists will be able to check the alignment for you.

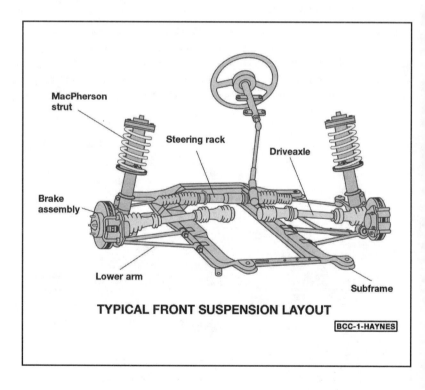

TYPICAL FRONT SUSPENSION LAYOUT

BCC-1-HAYNES

Steering

The steering's job is obvious, but steering systems have to be carefully designed to work in conjunction with the suspension. The steering system must allow the driver to keep the car pointing straight-ahead, even when hitting bumps at high speed, and the driver must be able to steer the car without too much effort.

When the steering wheel is turned, if the front wheels both turn through exactly the same angle, the tires will tend to scrub and wear out very quickly. This is because for the car to turn in a circle, the wheel on the inside of the turn needs to turn through a larger angle than the wheel on the outside of the turn. The steering and front suspension are designed to allow this to happen.

Many cars are equipped with power steering, to reduce the effort required to turn the steering wheel.

Most power steering systems use hydraulic pressure to increase the effort applied by the driver. An engine-driven pump supplies the hydraulic pressure. The system has to be carefully designed so that the amount of assistance is proportional to the amount of effort applied by the driver, and the driver can still "feel" what's happening to the front wheels.

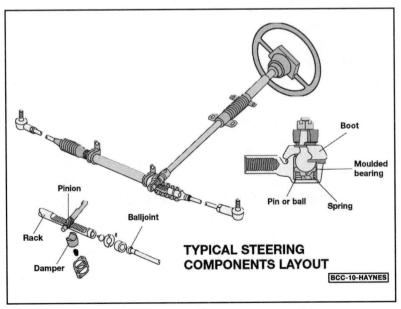

Boot

Moulded bearing

Pin or ball

Spring

Pinion

Balljoint

Rack

Damper

TYPICAL STEERING COMPONENTS LAYOUT

BCC-10-HAYNES

Steering problems

Basically, the same comments made under "Suspension problems" apply to the steering. The most common problem is poor front wheel alignment, which can cause tire wear.

Worn steering components can cause excessive free play at the steering wheel, and if you notice this problem, it should be dealt with as soon as possible.

Problems with power steering are usually due to leaks or air in the hydraulic system, or an incorrectly adjusted or broken pump drivebelt. If the power steering fails, the steering will still work, but the steering wheel will be harder to turn.

If you think there may be a problem with the steering, have it checked as soon as possible - never take any risks where the steering is concerned.

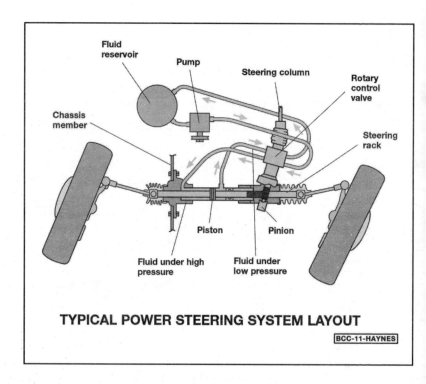

TYPICAL POWER STEERING SYSTEM LAYOUT

BCC-11-HAYNES

Brakes

Early cars had mechanical (cable- or rod-operated) brakes. As braking technology improved, hydraulic braking systems were introduced. All modern cars have hydraulic brakes.

The hydraulic system multiplies the pressure applied to the brake pedal, to give a much higher pressure at each brake. Hydraulic fluid can't be compressed. So, if the brake pedal operates a piston inside a master cylinder full of fluid connected to one end of a line (also full of fluid), this will move a second piston at the other end of the line, which can apply the brake. When a car is braking,

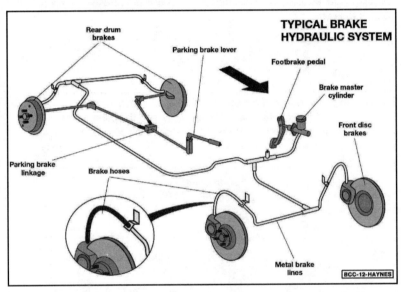

TYPICAL BRAKE HYDRAULIC SYSTEM

Rear drum brakes

Parking brake lever

Footbrake pedal

Brake master cylinder

Front disc brakes

Parking brake linkage

Brake hoses

Metal brake lines

BCC-12-HAYNES

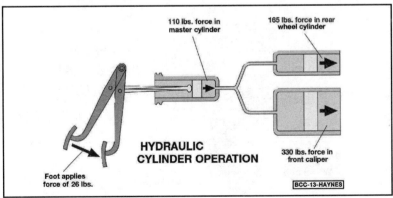

110 lbs. force in master cylinder

165 lbs. force in rear wheel cylinder

HYDRAULIC CYLINDER OPERATION

330 lbs. force in front caliper

Foot applies force of 26 lbs.

BCC-13-HAYNES

about two-thirds of its weight acts on the front wheels, so the front brakes normally have bigger pistons than the rear ones.

If there's a leak in the hydraulic system, the fluid can escape when the pedal is pushed, so the brakes won't work properly. As a safety measure the hydraulic system is split into two separate circuits, with two pedal-operated pistons in a common master cylinder. Usually, each circuit operates one front brake and the diagonally-opposite rear brake, so that if one of the circuits develops a leak, the car will still stop in a straight line. Some systems are split front and rear, one circuit operating both front brakes, the other operating both rear brakes.

Disc brakes

Front disc brakes are used on all modern cars, and disc brakes are also often used at the rear.

A disc brake assembly consists of a caliper and a disc. The caliper incorporates one or two hydraulic cylinders and pistons and carries two brake pads. The caliper straddles the disc, and is mounted on a fixed part of the front suspension. The disc is fixed to the rotating hub which turns with the wheel.

Each brake pad consists of a metal back plate, with friction material bonded to it. Eventually the friction material will wear away, and the pads will have to be replaced. For more information on disc brake pad replacement, purchase a repair manual for your particular vehicle.

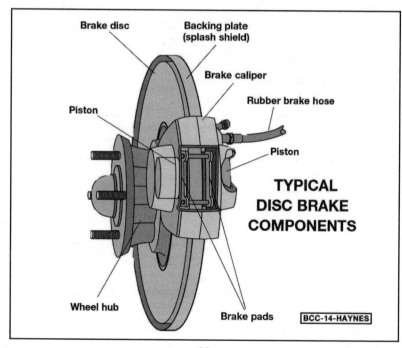

Brake disc

Backing plate
(splash shield)

Brake caliper

Rubber brake hose

Piston

Piston

**TYPICAL
DISC BRAKE
COMPONENTS**

Wheel hub

Brake pads

BCC-14-HAYNES

Drum brakes

Rear drum brakes are used on many modern cars, and on older cars they were used at the front as well.

A drum brake assembly consists of a wheel cylinder, two brake shoes, a back plate and a drum. The drum is fixed to the rotating hub which turns with the wheel. The brake shoes fit inside the drum, and are curved, with friction material on their outer faces. The shoes are mounted on the back plate, which is itself mounted on a fixed part of the rear suspension. One end of each shoe rests against an anchor point, which acts as a pivot. The other end is pushed outward by the piston in the wheel cylinder when the brake pedal is pressed, and contacts the inner surface of the drum, braking the drum and wheel. When the brakes are released, return springs stretched between the two shoes pull them away from the drum, which allows the drum and the wheel to turn freely. The brake shoe friction material will wear down in use and the shoes will require replacement. Obtain step-by-step instructions for this procedure in a repair manual for you particular vehicle, available at your local auto parts store.

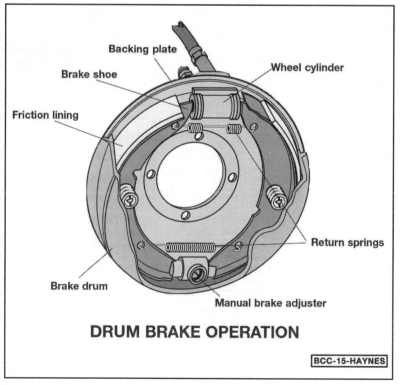

DRUM BRAKE OPERATION

BCC-15-HAYNES

Power brakes

A heavy car needs a high pedal pressure to give maximum braking power. Using a vacuum-operated booster reduces the pedal pressure exerted by the driver. The booster has a vacuum chamber connected to a vacuum source. A diaphragm in the booster chamber is connected to a pushrod, which operates the master cylinder pistons. When the brake pedal is pressed, air flows into the chamber behind the diaphragm, and because there's a vacuum on the other side, the air pushes the diaphragm forwards, operating the brakes. The amount of assistance is proportional to the pressure applied to the brake pedal.

If the booster develops a fault, the brakes will still work, but the driver will have to press the pedal much harder to achieve the same result.

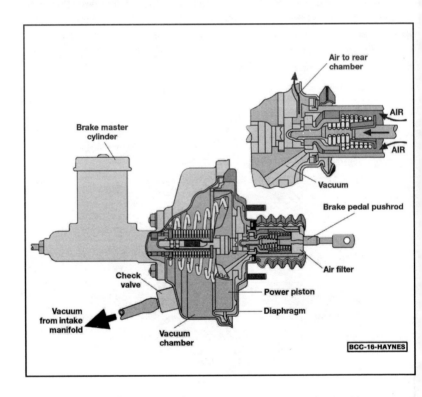

Anti-lock Braking Systems (ABS)

Anti-lock Braking Systems (ABS) are designed to stop wheels from locking under heavy braking. Some systems, mainly the early types, work only on the front wheels, but most systems work on all four wheels.

ABS works by detecting when a particular wheel is about to lock. It then reduces the hydraulic pressure applied to that wheel's brake, releasing it just before the wheel locks, and then re-applying it.

The system consists of a hydraulic unit, which contains various solenoid valves and an electric fluid return pump, four wheel sensors, and an electronic control unit (ECU). The solenoids in the hydraulic unit are controlled by the ECU, which receives signals from the four wheel sensors.

If the ECU senses that a wheel is about to lock, it operates the relevant solenoid valve in the hydraulic unit, which isolates that brake from the master cylinder. If the wheel sensor detects that the wheel is still about to lock, the ECU switches on the fluid return pump in the hydraulic unit and pumps the fluid back from the brake to the master cylinder, releasing the

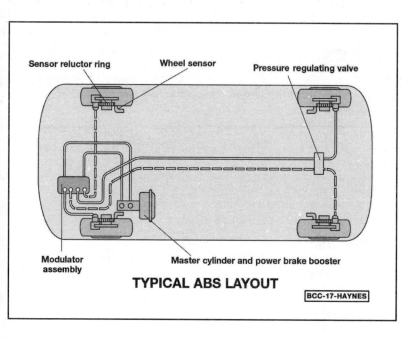

TYPICAL ABS LAYOUT

BCC-17-HAYNES

brake. Once the speed of the wheel returns to normal, the return pump stops and the solenoid valve opens, allowing fluid pressure back to the brake, and so the brake is re-applied. This whole cycle can be repeated many times a second. The rapid variations in fluid pressure cause pulses in the hydraulic circuit, and these can be felt through the brake pedal.

The wheel sensors are usually mounted on a fixed part of the suspension, and use a toothed rotor fixed to the wheel hub to monitor the speed of the wheel.

The system relies totally on electrical signals. If an inaccurate signal or a battery problem is detected, the ABS is automatically shut down, and a warning light on the instrument panel will come on. Normal braking will always be available whether or not the ABS is working.

ABS cannot work miracles, and the basic laws of physics will still apply: stopping distances will always be greater on slippery surfaces. The greatest benefit of ABS is being able to brake hard in an emergency without having to worry about correcting a skid.

If you have any problems with an ABS, always consult an authorized dealer.

Parking brake

The parking brake is usually operated by pulling a lever. The parking brake usually works on the rear wheels, although a few cars have a front wheel parking brake.

If rear drum brakes are used, the parking brake operates the same shoes as the service brake, using cables and levers to push the shoes against the drum.

Several different parking brake systems are used on cars with disc brakes. Some systems use small additional drum brakes, some use two additional pads, and others use a mechanical linkage to operate the main caliper pistons.

Almost all types of parking brakes have adjustment to allow for friction material wear and parking brake cable stretch.

Common problems and easy fixes

Most common breakdown problems

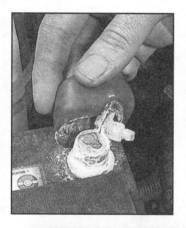

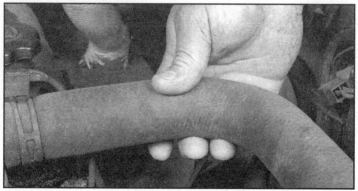

5 easy steps to prevent the most common breakdown problems

Battery

Probably the number one breakdown problem is related to the battery. If you turn the key in the ignition and get nothing at all or a clicking sound, chances are you have a battery problem. Assuming you have not drained the battery by leaving the lights or an accessory on (in which case a Jump

Start should get you going again), either the battery has failed due to old age or the cables are loose or corroded. Whenever you are under the hood, check that the battery cables are tight and clean. Remove any white, fluffy deposits on the terminals and cable ends and replace the battery at the first sign of weakness (especially after a few years of use) to prevent this common breakdown problem. See *Battery maintenance* for more information.

Oil

Check the oil level regularly, and replace the oil and filter at the recommended intervals (make sure you use the correct type of oil for your engine). Oil is the engine's blood supply - without oil, the engine will die! If the oil pressure warning light on the dashboard comes on, stop the engine immediately. See

Fluid checking and *Engine oil and filter change* for more information.

Rubber hoses and drivebelts

Check all the engine's rubber hoses for damage and deterioration, and make sure all the hose clamps are tight - leaking hoses can cause serious problems. Regularly check the engine accessory drivebelt(s) and, where applicable, have the engine timing belt replaced at the intervals recommended by the manufacturer. For additional information, see *Checking underhood hoses* later in this guide.

Gasoline

Avoid running your vehicle when the fuel level is extremely low. If you run out of fuel, dirt or sediment from the bottom of the gas tank can be drawn into the fuel system, and although most cars have a fuel filter, blockages or contamination from very fine particles can still cause trouble.

Coolant

Check the coolant level regularly, and keep it at the proper level. If you've got a leak, have it fixed as soon as possible. Keep an eye on the temperature gauge, and if the engine overheats, stop and let it cool down before continuing. Overheating can cause serious engine damage.

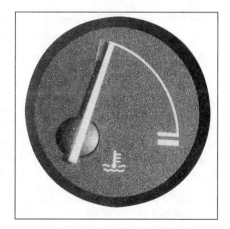

How to change a tire

Changing a tire is straightforward provided you know where the tools and spare wheel are kept, and how to use the jack. If you've just bought the car, or if you've never changed a tire before, it's worth practicing at home, then you'll know exactly what to do if you get a flat tire.

First make sure that the car is parked safely away from traffic. If you're at the side of a busy road, and you can't move the car, it's safer to call for assistance rather than risk an accident. Stop the car, switch on the hazard warning lights, and set up your warning triangle if you have one.

1 Apply the parking brake, engage first gear (set automatic transmission to "P"). As an extra safety precaution, go to the wheel diagonally opposite the one to be changed and block it in place, as shown.

2 Get out the spare wheel, vehicle jack and lug wrench. They are generally located in the luggage area, under a cover in the floor (check your Owner's manual for details).

3 Where applicable, remove the wheel trim/cover. Use the lug wrench to loosen each wheel bolt/nut on the affected wheel by about half a turn.

4 Engage the jack head in the jacking point nearest the affected wheel (check your Owner's manual for details). Slide the spare wheel part way under the car, near the wheel to be removed, but out of the way of the jack (this is a safety measure). Raise the jack until the wheel is an inch or two off the ground.

Sometimes it's difficult to loosen the lug bolts or nuts. You can buy a lug wrench with an extending handle to make things easier, or alternatively, you can carry a length of metal tube to fit over the lug wrench for more leverage.

5 Remove the wheel bolts/nuts, and lift off the wheel. Drag out the spare wheel and slide the removed wheel under the car in its place.

6 Fit the spare wheel, then install the bolts/nuts, and tighten them until they're just holding the wheel firmly. Remove the wheel from under the car, then lower the jack, and remove it from under the car.

8 When you've finished, stow the removed wheel and the tools back in their correct locations. Check the pressure in the "new" tire, with your gauge or at the nearest gas station. It's important to get the flat tire repaired or replaced as soon as possible - don't put it off!

7 Tighten one lug bolt/nut securely, using the lug wrench, then tighten the one diagonally opposite. Tighten the other bolts/nuts in the same way, then install the wheel trim, where applicable.

INSTALLING A WHEEL

Positioning a wheel can be tricky as you have to support its weight at the same time. If you find this difficult, try resting the wheel on your foot and using it to help you maneuver the wheel into position.

SPACE-SAVER
SPARE TIRES

These tires are narrower than normal tires, and are often inflated to a different pressure. There are usually speed and mileage restrictions marked on the tire, or printed in the Owner's manual - make sure you observe these restrictions. If you install a "space-saver" tire, have the flat tire repaired and installed as soon as possible.

What's that noise?

A strange noise could spell trouble, or it could just be an annoying distraction - so how do you tell? Here's a guide to help you to identify noises and decide what to do about them, even if you just want to describe the problem to a mechanic. Additional information on identifying common problems can be found in a repair manual for your particular vehicle. These repair manuals are available at auto parts stores and will also give step-by-step instructions on repairing these faults.

Noise	Possible cause	Remarks
NOISES FROM THE EXHAUST		
Light "puffing" or blowing noise when accelerating or decelerating, or when engine is idling	Small hole or crack in exhaust system	Repair temporarily with exhaust putty. Go to exhaust specialist for advice.
Sudden increase in noise, especially when accelerating and decelerating	Hole or crack in exhaust system, or failed muffler	Repair temporarily with exhaust bandage. Go to exhaust specialist for advice.
Metallic rattling or thumping over bumps, or when accelerating and decelerating	Loose or broken exhaust mounting.	Repair temporarily with wire. Go to exhaust specialist for advice.
NOISES FROM THE BRAKES		
Light squeaking when applying brakes gently for the first time of the day	Normal characteristic of disc brakes	Could be normal.
Squealing whenever brakes are applied	Could be first sign of excessively worn brake friction material	Ask your mechanic to check - possibly cured by applying special brake grease or anti-squeal compound to the brake pad backing plates. Replace brake pads or shoes if required.
Deep metallic scraping when brakes are applied, or when the brakes aren't in use	Excessively worn brake components Trapped stone or dirt between brake disc and pad	Have your mechanic investigate without delay before further damage occurs.
Chattering or tapping when brakes are applied	Contaminated brake friction material	Damaged brake discs or drums. Have your mechanic investigate without delay.

COMMON PROBLEMS AND EASY FIXES

Noise	Possible cause	Remarks
NOISES FROM THE SUSPENSION		
Clunks or rattles when driving over bumps	Worn or damaged suspension or steering components Loose or broken exhaust mounting	Probably not urgent, but have your mechanic investigate before too long.
Rumbling, growling or clicking noises when turning corners	Worn wheel bearing(s) Worn CV joint (front-wheel-drive cars)	Probably not urgent, but may cause further damage if neglected.
"Hissing" noise when driving slowly over bumps	Badly worn shock absorbers	Drive carefully until new shock absorbers have been installed - handling and ride may be poor.
Low-speed clicking noise	Object trapped in wheel hubcap	Remove object from hubcap
NOISES FROM THE ENGINE COMPARTMENT		
Squealing	Loose or worn auxiliary drivebelt	Probably not urgent, but get it fixed before it breaks.
Continuous hum or whine	Auxiliary drivebelt or timing belt too tight Alternator, water pump or power steering pump worn	Probably not urgent, but get it fixed before it gets worse.
Rhythmic slapping when the engine is cold	"Piston slap"	Not a problem as long as it stops when the engine warms up.
Light tapping from the top of the engine	Valve clearances incorrect (too large)	Not urgent, but have them adjusted at the next service.
Rhythmic metallic thumping or thudding	Worn engine bearings	May be a serious problem. Have it investigated without delay.
High-pitched metallic rattle when engine is under load (accelerating or driving uphill)	Engine "pinging" or "pre-ignition" (poor quality fuel or wrong fuel type, or ignition system problem)	Drive gently until you can fill up with good fuel or have the ignition system checked.

COMMON PROBLEMS AND EASY FIXES

Noise	Possible cause	Remarks
NOISES FROM THE TRANSMISSION		
Whine or howl from manual transmission in neutral, softens or disappears when clutch pedal is depressed	Worn transmission bearing	You can still drive, but have it fixed before it gets much worse.
Whine or howl from manual transmission when clutch pedal is depressed, softens or disappears when pedal is released	Worn clutch release bearing	You can still drive, but have it fixed before it gets much worse.
Squealing from manual transmission as clutch is engaged or released	Incorrectly adjusted clutch Worn clutch	If adjustment doesn't cure the problem, have it fixed before it gets worse.
Whine or howl from automatic transmission in neutral	Low transmission fluid level Worn or damaged transmission	Check the fluid level. If that's OK, have the transmission checked without delay.
Howl or whine when accelerating or decelerating	Low transmission oil/fluid level Worn bearing in transmission Worn or damaged differential	Check the oil level. If that's OK, you can probably carry on driving for a while, but have the transmission checked before something breaks.
Grinding sound from manual transmission when changing gear	Incorrectly adjusted clutch Worn synchromesh units in transmission Badly worn gears	If clutch adjustment doesn't cure it, you probably need a new transmission.

What to do if the engine overheats

Cars most often overheat when stuck in traffic - keep an eye on the temperature gauge. Overheating can cause serious and expensive engine damage, so watch for the warning signs!

If the temperature gauge is working, the first sign will be the gauge needle creeping towards the red. Sometimes a temperature warning light is installed. If you notice either of these signs, move the heater control to maximum immediately, and switch the heater blower motor to maximum - this will get rid of some of the heat from the engine. If the temperature doesn't drop, or keeps going up, pull over in a safe place and stop the engine.

In extreme cases, the first sign of overheating may be steam coming from under the hood. Pull over and stop as soon as possible. Don't open the hood until the steam stops.

If no steam is coming from under the hood, open the hood to help the heat escape, and wait for the engine to cool down!

A very hot engine takes time to cool, and you'll have to wait at least half-an-hour before the temperature drops to normal.

Check under the car for coolant leakage - coolant is usually brightly colored (often green or orange), and will probably be steaming if it's hot!

If there's a leak, call for assistance.

When the engine has cooled, check the coolant level - if there's been no leakage, and no steam, the level will probably be above the "maximum" mark (hot coolant expands). If the coolant level is OK, and there's no leakage, it's safe to keep driving, but keep an eye on the temperature gauge!

If the level is low, add coolant. You can use plain water in an emergency. If almost all the coolant has been lost, don't fill the system with cold water while the engine is hot, as this might cause engine damage.

What causes overheating?

Apart from simply getting too hot on a summer's day in traffic, here are the most common causes of engine overheating:

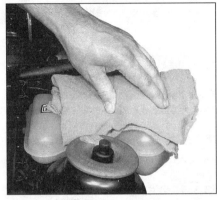

- Low coolant level

- Faulty cooling fan

- Leakage

- Faulty water pump

- Broken water pump drivebelt (where applicable)

- Blown cylinder head gasket

Place a large rag over the coolant filler cap, and release the cap very slowly to allow the pressure to escape - hot coolant and steam cause severe burns!

Refer to a model specific repair manual for diagnosis and repair of these components.

WARNING

Never remove the reservoir cap while the engine is hot - (you could be severely burned). Unscrew the cap slowly and allow any pressure to escape. Wash off any accidental splashes from your skin, and from the car's paint - it can cause paint damage.

Leaks

A leak may show up as a stain under your car, or you may need to add fluid frequently. So how do you tell if a leak is serious, or something you can live with for a while?

BRAKE FLUID

Symptoms

Brake fluid is clear, thin and almost watery. Old brake fluid gradually darkens. Compare the leak with the contents of the brake fluid reservoir. Leaks usually come from around the wheels, the brake line connections under the car, or the brake master cylinder in the engine compartment.

Is it OK to drive the car?

DON'T drive the car if you think there might be a brake fluid leak.

Is it easy to fix?

Disassembly will be required to fix this - refer to a repair manual or call for help.

CLUTCH FLUID

Symptoms

Leaks usually come from hydraulic line connections, or from failed seals in the hydraulic components.

Is it OK to drive the car?

It's OK to drive with a minor leak, but if you lose much of the fluid, the clutch won't work.

Is it easy to fix?

You might be able to fix a leaky fluid line connection by tightening it. The leak could be due to a failed fluid seal in one of the clutch hydraulic components. Disassembly will be required to fix this - refer to a repair manual or call for help.

GASOLINE

Warning: *Gasoline is extremely flammable, so take extra precautions when you work on any part of the fuel system. Don't smoke or allow open flames or bare light bulbs near the work area, and don't work in a garage where a gas-type appliance (such as a water heater or a clothes dryer) is present. Since gasoline is carcinogenic, wear fuel-resistant gloves when there's a possibility of being exposed to fuel, and if you spill any on your skin, rinse it off immediately with soap and water. Mop up any spills immediately and do not store fuel-soaked rags where they could ignite. The fuel system on fuel-injected vehicles is under constant pressure, so, if any fuel lines are to be disconnected, the pressure must be relieved first (refer to a model-specific repair manual for the proper procedure). When you perform any kind of work on the fuel system, wear safety glasses and have a Class B type fire extinguisher on hand.*

Symptoms

Gasoline has a strong and distinctive smell, so a leak should be obvious. If you've just filled up with gasoline on a hot day, and the car's standing in the sun, the gasoline may expand, and leak out through the fuel tank vent. Gasoline can also leak if you park a car with a full tank on a steep slope.

If the leak's not due to either of the above causes, have it investigated immediately.

Is it OK to drive the car?

DON'T drive the car until the leak's been fixed.

Is it easy to fix?

If the leak's coming from a hose connection, you might be able to fix it by tightening the connection (or hose clamp). If not, refer to a repair manual or call for help.

ENGINE OIL

Symptoms

Engine oil is usually black, unless it's recently been changed. Clean oil is usually clear or tan. Compare the leak with the oil on the end of the oil level dipstick. The most common sources of leaks are the oil drain plug, the oil filter, and the oil pan gasket under the engine.

Is it OK to drive the car?

You can drive with a minor oil leak, but keep an eye on the oil level.

Is it easy to fix?

If the leak's coming from the oil drain plug or the filter, try tightening the plug or filter (as applicable). If the leak's coming from anywhere else, have it checked as soon as possible.

COMMON PROBLEMS AND EASY FIXES

WATER

If a leak looks like clear water, and your car has air conditioning, it may not be a leak, but condensation from the air conditioning. A lot of condensation can be produced on a hot day, which may look like a major leak.

Also see "Coolant" and "Washer fluid".

AUTOMATIC TRANSMISSION FLUID

Symptoms

The fluid is usually dark red. Compare the leak with the fluid on the end of the transmission fluid level dipstick. Leaks usually come from the transmission case, or from fluid lines running to the fluid cooler (this could be mounted on the transmission, or incorporated in the radiator).

Is it OK to drive the car?

You can drive with a minor leak, but keep an eye on the fluid level.

Is it easy to fix?

You might be able to fix a leaky connection by tightening it. Any other leaks should be checked out by a mechanic.

MANUAL TRANSMISSION OR DIFFERENTIAL FLUID

Symptoms

The fluid is usually a tan color or reddish-pink, although old fluid may darken. Some transmission fluids are thicker than engine oil, and sometimes have a distinctive smell, especially when hot.

Is it OK to drive the car?

You can drive with a minor leak, but if the oil level gets too low, it can cause serious transmission damage.

Is it easy to fix?

Most leaks are due to failed gaskets or oil seals, so disassembly is usually required to fix the leak - refer to a repair manual or get a mechanic to have a look as soon as you can.

WASHER FLUID

Symptoms

Washer fluid usually contains a blue dye. The leak could be due to a poor hose connection, or a leaky washer pump seal in the fluid reservoir.

Is it OK to drive the car?

Yes!

Is it easy to fix?

Yes, but it might be tricky to get to the fluid hoses and reservoir.

POWER STEERING FLUID

Symptoms

The fluid is usually clear or red. Compare the leak with the contents of the power steering fluid reservoir. Leaks usually come from fluid line connections, the power steering pump, or the steering gear.

Is it OK to drive the car?

You can drive with a minor leak, but keep an eye on the fluid level.

Is it easy to fix?

To fix a leaky fluid line connection, try tightening it. If the pump or steering gear is leaking, refer to a repair manual or get advice from a mechanic as soon as possible.

COMMON PROBLEMS AND EASY FIXES

ENGINE COOLANT

Warning: *Do not allow coolant to come in contact with your skin or painted surfaces of the vehicle. Rinse off spills immediately with plenty of water. Coolant is highly toxic if ingested. Never leave coolant lying around in an open container or in puddles on the floor; children and pets are attracted by its sweet smell and may drink it. Coolant is also flammable, so don't store or use it near open flames. Check with local authorities about disposing of used coolant. Many communities have collection centers which will see that coolant is disposed of safely. Never dump used coolant on the ground or into drains.*

Note: *Non-toxic coolant is available at auto parts store. Although the coolant is non-toxic when fresh, proper disposal is still required.*

Symptoms

Coolant (also called antifreeze) usually contains a bright-colored dye (green or orange), and has a strong, sweet smell. Old coolant may be rusty or dirty brown, and there may be a white crystalline deposit around the leak. Leaks usually come from a hose, the radiator, or the heater inside the car (you'll smell coolant when you switch the heater on).

Is it OK to drive the car?

You can drive with a minor leak, but if you lose too much coolant, the engine could overheat.

Is it easy to fix?

Sometimes you can stop a leak by tightening up a hose clamp. If a hose is split, you might be able to make an emergency repair using high-temperature duct tape. If the radiator or heater is leaking, you may be able to fix it temporarily by using a radiator sealant.

Do-it-yourself maintenance

The following procedures are a good general guide to vehicle maintenance. You should seriously consider purchasing a repair manual written specifically for your make/model vehicle. This will provide comprehensive maintenance and repair procedures. These manuals are commonly available at your local auto parts store.

FLUID CHECKING
Engine oil

If the engine oil level gets too low, it could cause serious engine damage, so it's vital to check the oil level regularly. Check the engine oil level once a week, or before a long trip. The oil level should be between the upper and

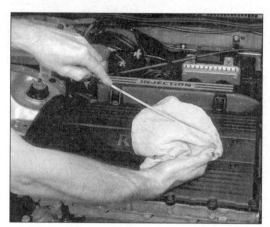

lower marks on the dipstick.

The engine oil and filter should be changed every 3000 miles or three months. For information on changing the engine oil, see *Engine oil and filter change*, later in this section.

Brake fluid

If the brake fluid level gets too low, the brakes will work poorly, or not at all. Regular checking of the fluid level will warn you if a leak's developing. The fluid level falls gradually as the brake pads wear, but if you're adding fluid regularly, there must be a leak - stop driving the car until the leak's been found and fixed.

1 Make sure the car is level, then wipe the brake fluid reservoir clean. The level must be kept between the "MAX" and "MIN" marks.

Check the brake fluid level once a week, or before a long trip.

Some manufacturers recommend specific intervals for brake fluid replacement (changing). This practice may add life to your brake hydraulic system.

2 If topping up is needed, unscrew and remove the reservoir cap. Usually, the inside of the cap fits down into the fluid, so pull it out slowly, and place it on a piece of clean cloth to catch drips.

3 Top up to the "MAX" mark. Use a good quality brake fluid which meets the standard recommended by the manufacturer (usually DOT 3 - it will be marked on the container). Always use new fluid from a freshly-opened container.

4 Install the reservoir cap and discard the cloth.

WARNING

Brake fluid is poisonous. It's also flammable, and acts as a very effective paint stripper. Wash any splashes off skin or paint right away with lots of clean water.

Coolant

Warning: *Do not allow coolant to come in contact with your skin or painted surfaces of the vehicle. Rinse off spills immediately with plenty of water. Coolant is highly toxic if ingested. Never leave coolant lying around in an open container or in puddles on the floor; children and pets are attracted by its sweet smell and may drink it. Coolant is also flammable, so don't store or use it near open flames. Check with local authorities about disposing of used coolant. Many communities have collection centers which will see that coolant is disposed of safely. Never dump used coolant on the ground or into drains.*

Note: *Non-toxic coolant is available at auto parts store. Although the coolant is non-toxic when fresh, proper disposal is still required.*

The coolant is pumped through the engine, and cools it by means of the radiator. If the level gets too low, it could cause overheating and serious engine damage. It's normal to have to add coolant occasionally, but the need for regular additions suggests that there's a leak or some other problem which should be fixed before it gets serious. Make sure you use the right type of coolant when adding - some cars use coolant which cannot be mixed with other types (check in your car's owner's manual for details).

Check the level once a week, or before a long trip. The coolant should be changed at the manufacturer's recommended intervals. A few manufacturers use "lifetime" coolant, which is designed to last the life of the car - check in your car's owner's manual for details.

The coolant reservoir may be transparent, or it may have a level indicator inside, which is visible once the cap has been removed.

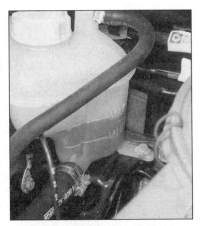

1 Check that the level is up to the internal indicator or between the "MIN" and "MAX" marks. If you need to remove the reservoir cap, carefully unscrew the cap and check the level.

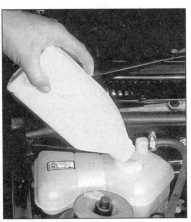

2 If the level's low, add a 50/50 mixture of water and antifreeze (or clean tap water in an emergency) to bring the level up to the appropriate mark. Don't overfill.

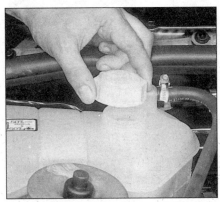

3 Install the cap tightly afterwards, and wipe away any spills.

WARNING

Never remove the reservoir cap while the engine is hot - (you could be severely burned). Unscrew the cap slowly and allow any pressure to escape. Wash off any accidental splashes from your skin, and from the car's paint - it can cause paint damage.

Power steering fluid

If your car has power steering and the fluid level's low, there may be a hissing or squealing sound as the steering wheel is turned. If the level is very low, or the system's leaking, the power steering system may be damaged, and the steering wheel will be harder to turn.

Many power steering systems use automatic transmission fluid, but you should always check with your car's owner's manual - different types of systems use different fluids, and you could cause damage if you use the wrong fluid.

Have the system checked for leaks if you need to add fluid regularly.

Check the power steering fluid level once a week, or before a long trip.

The power steering fluid reservoir may be transparent with level markings on the outside, or it may have a level dipstick on the filler cap.

1 If you need to remove the filler cap to check the level, wipe around the cap first, then unscrew the cap.

2 Read off the fluid level, and add if necessary. Sometimes there may be "HOT" and "COLD" level markings for use depending on whether the engine's hot or cold - the level should be up to the relevant mark.

3 If the level's low, wipe around the filler cap, then remove it, if not already done, and add to the correct mark. Don't overfill. Install the filler cap tightly afterwards.

Windshield washer fluid

You can use plain water in the washer reservoir, but water can freeze in cold climates. Washer fluid, usually blue in color, contains alcohol as an anti-freeze. Washer fluid is available at auto parts store. Note the directions on the container as to the quantity to add.

Check the washer fluid level once a week, or before a long trip. Many people find it convenient to add the washer fluid when they fill up with fuel.

The windshield washer reservoir is usually located in the engine compartment. If your car has headlight washers, the headlight washers normally use fluid from the windshield washer fluid reservoir, although on some cars a separate reservoir may be used. Similarly, if a rear washer system is used, there may be a combined windshield/rear fluid reservoir, or there may be a separate rear washer fluid reservoir (sometimes behind a panel in the luggage area).

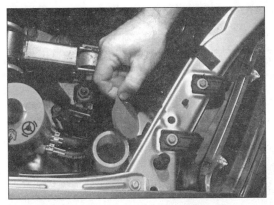

1 If you need to add fluid, wipe away any dirt from around the filler neck, then pull off the filler cap.

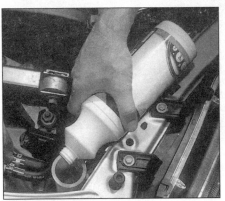

2 Fill the reservoir, then install the cap firmly, and wipe away any spillage. A funnel can make the job easier.

3 You can clear a blocked washer jet by poking the fine nozzle gently with a pin. You can also use the pin to swivel the "eyeball" so that the jet is aimed correctly - but don't break the pin off in the nozzle.

WARNING

Never use engine antifreeze in the washer system - it's not only hazardous to health, but it will also damage the car's paint and trim. Use a good quality washer fluid.

Automatic transmission fluid

Note: *Illustrated here is a typical procedure for checking automatic transmission fluid. Your car may have a different procedure, which will be in your owner's manual. Follow your owner's manual procedure wherever it differs from the information printed here.*

If the automatic transmission fluid level gets low, the transmission may not work properly - low fluid level is a common source of problems with auto-

matic transmissions. If the level gets too low, it could damage the transmission. There are several different types of transmission fluid, and it's essential that you use the right one, so you'll need to check with your car manufacturer's information, or an authorized dealer. If frequent fluid addition is needed, have the cause found and fixed without delay.

1 With the engine running and the parking brake on, press the brake pedal, and move the gear selector lever through all the gear positions, starting and ending in "P". Let the engine idle for one minute then, with the engine still running, pull out the dipstick. Wipe the dipstick with a clean cloth, and push it carefully back into its tube.

2 Pull out the dipstick again then check the fluid level. Sometimes, you'll find the dipstick has two sets of markings, one for checking the fluid hot (or at high temperature, eg, 160-degrees F), and one for checking cold (or at low temperature, eg, 70-degrees F).

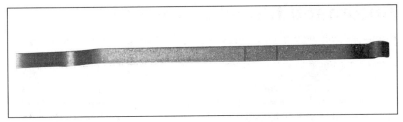

3 Read off the fluid level, and if more fluid is needed, stop the engine.

The automatic transmission fluid should be checked at the manufacturer's recommended intervals (at least every 3000 miles or 3 months).

The following advice is only a guide - you need to check your car's owner's manual to see exactly how to check the automatic transmission fluid level, but most use the same technique, with a level dipstick which fits inside a tube attached to the transmission. The level is usually checked with the transmission warm, after a short drive.

Have the transmission fluid changed at the manufacturer's recommended intervals (usually around every 30,000 miles).

4 Usually, fluid is added through the dipstick tube, so you'll need a bottle with a tube, or a clean funnel, to stop spills. Don't overfill, and be very careful not to introduce dust or dirt into the transmission.

5 Re-check the level with the engine running, and finally reinsert the dipstick when the level's correct.

Clutch fluid

Some cars with manual transmissions have a hydraulic clutch. Sometimes, the clutch hydraulic system may be sealed, or may share a common reservoir with the braking system - alternatively, there may be a separate clutch fluid reservoir (check your car's owner's manual for details). If the fluid level is low, there must be a leak - a bad leak will cause the clutch to malfunction, so have the system checked if you need to add fluid regularly.

Check the clutch fluid level once a week, or before a long trip.

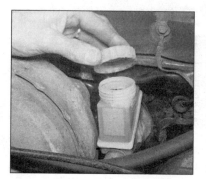

2 If the level is low, unscrew and remove the reservoir cap.

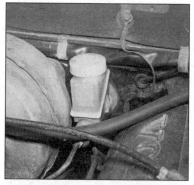

1 Make sure the car's parked on level ground, then wipe the clutch fluid reservoir clean if it's dirty. The fluid level must always be kept between the "MAX" and "MIN" marks - if there are no level markings, the fluid level should normally be up to the lower edge of the reservoir fillerneck.

4 Install the reservoir cap when you've finished.

3 Add only new brake fluid. Use a good quality brake fluid which meets the standard recommended by the manufacturer (usually DOT 3 - it will be marked on the container). Always use new fluid from a freshly-opened container - using old brake fluid could result in the clutch not working properly.

WARNING

Hydraulic fluid is poisonous. It's also flammable, and acts as a very effective paint stripper. Wash any splashes off skin or paint right away with lots of clean water.

Tuning up

A tune-up means that the engine fuel and ignition system settings are checked to make sure that they're within the manufacturer's recommended limits. On older cars, a shop can check, and, if necessary, adjust the engine idle speed, the fuel/air mixture and the ignition timing, but on most modern cars, these settings are controlled by the engine management system and can't be adjusted (although they can still be checked if the right equipment is available).

During the tune-up, it's also a good idea to perform other routine maintenance.

Provided your car is regularly serviced, tuning up isn't very often needed on a modern car, because there's not much to go wrong. For more information on tuning up your car, purchase a repair manual on your particular vehicle.

These are the main checks which are normally done:

- Check the engine oil level
- Check the coolant level
- Replace the air filter
- Check the fuel filter (where applicable)
- Replace the spark plugs
- Check the battery
- Check the ignition and fuel system wiring and hoses
- A shop may be able to check the engine idle speed, the fuel mixture and the ignition timing, but on most modern engines, these settings are controlled by the engine management system, and can't be adjusted.

Interior ventilation filter

Some cars have an interior ventilation filter to filter the air which goes into the heating/ventilation system. The filter will stop pollen and dust from the atmosphere being drawn into the car's interior.

The filter should be replaced at the manufacturer's recommended intervals (usually around 15,000 miles or yearly). For more specific information on the filter location and replacement procedure, purchase a repair manual for your particular vehicle at your local auto parts store.

1 Interior ventilation filters come in various shapes and sizes, and you might have to remove surrounding trim panels for access to the filter.

2 The filters are usually located under the cowl panel at the back of the engine compartment, or behind the glove box, inside the car.

Air filter

The filter stops dirt and dust from being sucked into the engine. If the element's very dirty or blocked, the engine won't run properly, and the fuel consumption might be higher than normal. If the filter is missing or damaged, dirt

Air filters are usually housed in a rectangular box next to the engine, or a round housing on top of the engine. Sometimes you may have to unclip a hose or disconnect an electrical connector plug before you can remove the air filter cover

1 Release the clips and/or unscrew the securing screws, then lift the cover from the air filter housing.

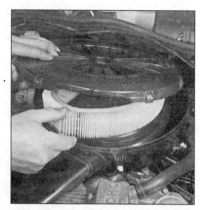

2 Lift out the air filter, noting which way it's installed (some filters install either way up). Make sure the new filter's the same.

may be sucked into the engine, causing expensive damage. When buying a new air filter, you'll need to know the model, engine size and year of manufacture of your car.

Replace the air filter at the manufacturer's recommended intervals, typically every 24,000 miles or two years.

3 Wipe out the housing and the cover using a clean cloth. Be careful not to get any dirt or dust into the air intake.

4 Install the new filter into the housing, making sure that it's the right way up, then install the cover and secure it with the clips and/or screws.

How to change spark plugs

You will need a set of new spark plugs, a spark plug socket, a spark plug adjustment tool and feeler gauges, a tube of anti-seize compound, and a length of rubber or plastic hose to fit over the end of the spark plugs (about six inches long).

Before you start, make sure the engine's cold and the ignition is turned off. Some vehicles require special tools or additional disassembly to reach the spark plugs. See a repair manual on your particular vehicle for details.

The spark plugs are located at the top of the engine, often at the front or back or, on some engines, at the center of the engine under a cover. Sometimes, you'll need to unbolt surrounding components for access to the plugs.

1 Work on one plug at a time, so you won't get the firing order confused. Gently twist and pull the spark plug wire - pull on the connector, not on the wire itself.

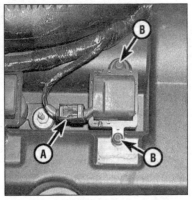

2 Many newer cars have no spark plug wires - the ignition coils are directly over the plugs. Disconnect the electrical connector(s) (A), then remove the bolt(s) (B) and pull off the coil.

3 If there's dirt around the plug, blow the dirt away, using the hose to concentrate and direct your breath. Then, using the spark plug socket, unscrew and remove the plug.

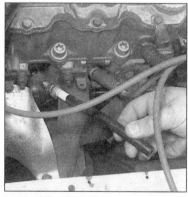

4 Using feeler gauges, make sure the new plug has the correct gap between the electrodes (refer to your car's owner's manual for this). The gap is important, and the engine won't run properly if it's wrong.

5 Rub a little anti-seize compound onto the threads of the new plug, then use the rubber hose to screw the plug into position. If the threads are crossed, the hose will slip, so you won't damage the threads. If the hose slips, remove the plug, and try again.

6 Screw the plug in as far as possible using the hose, then tighten it using the spark plug socket. Don't overtighten the plug.

7 Reconnect the wire, then repeat the steps for the other spark plugs in turn.

8 When you've finished, install any components you had to remove for access.

Drivebelts

Drivebelts are usually driven by a pulley on the end of the crankshaft and drive the engine accessories, such as the alternator, power steering and air conditioning compressor and, on some cars, the water pump. One drivebelt may drive all the accessories, or several separate drivebelts may be used.

Drivebelt inspection is part of the maintenance schedule on most cars, and you'll almost certainly have to renew the drivebelt(s) at some point if you keep the car for any length of time.

Buying a spare drivebelt

It's always best to carry the correct spare drivebelt for your particular car. You can buy replacement drivebelts from auto parts store. To help find the correct new belt, if possible take the old belt along with you. Drivebelts stretch in use, so don't worry if a new belt is slightly shorter than a used one.

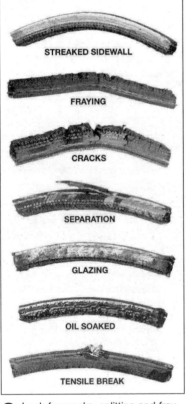

STREAKED SIDEWALL

FRAYING

CRACKS

SEPARATION

GLAZING

OIL SOAKED

TENSILE BREAK

1 It can be tricky to reach a drivebelt, and access may be easiest from under the car (you may have to unbolt covers for access). Check the whole length of the belt - you'll probably need to turn the engine. Usually, the easiest way to turn the engine is to use a wrench on the bolt or nut on the pulley end of the crankshaft.

2 Look for cracks, splitting and fraying on the surface of the belt, and check for signs of shiny patches. If you find any damage or wear, a new belt should be installed.

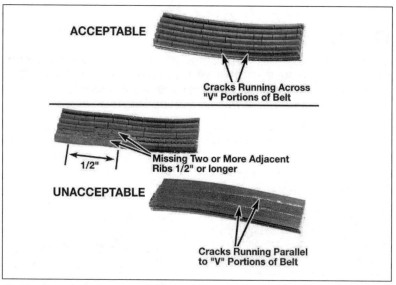

ACCEPTABLE

Cracks Running Across
"V" Portions of Belt

1/2"

Missing Two or More Adjacent
Ribs 1/2" or longer

UNACCEPTABLE

Cracks Running Parallel
to "V" Portions of Belt

3 Small cracks in the underside of a V-ribbed belt are acceptable - lengthwise cracks, or missing pieces that cause the belt to make noise, are cause for replacement

4 An automatic or a manually-adjustable tensioner may be used. A manually-adjustable belt may be adjusted by moving the component it drives (such as the alternator), or there may be a separate adjuster assembly.

6 A belt will squeal if it's too loose, especially when pulling away from a standstill. A belt that's too tight may "hum."

5 Most manufacturers specify a tension for each belt, but you should be able to tension a belt correctly by a little trial-and-error. The belt must be tight enough to stop slipping, but not so tight that it strains the accessories - if you can push the belt down by about 1/4 to 1/2-inch using light finger pressure at the middle of the longest belt run between the pulleys, this should be good enough for most engines.

Checking underhood hoses

High temperatures under the hood can cause the deterioration of the rubber and plastic hoses used for engine, accessory and emission systems operation. You can avoid a breakdown on the road with a periodic inspection for cracks, loose clamps, material hardening and leaks.

Check for a chafed area that could fail prematurely.

Check for a soft area indicating the hose has deteriorated inside.

Overtightening the clamp on a hardened hose will damage the hose and cause a leak.

Check each hose for swelling and oil-soaked ends. Cracks and breaks can be located by squeezing the hose.

Cooling system hoses

Carefully check the upper and lower radiator hoses along with the smaller diameter heater hoses. Inspect the entire length of each hose, replacing any that are cracked, swollen or deteriorated. Cracks may become more apparent when a hose is squeezed.

Check also that all hose connections are tight. Spring-type hose clamps can lose their tension over time, so replace them with the more reliable screw-type clamps when installing a new hose. A leak in the cooling system will usually show up as white or rust-colored deposits on the areas adjoining the leak.

Vacuum hoses

Vacuum hoses, especially those in the emissions system are color-coded or identified because various systems require hoses with different wall thickness for resistance to collapsing and high temperatures. Be sure any replacement hoses are made of the same material.

Often the only effective way to check a hose is to remove it. Be sure to label the hose and its attaching points to insure proper reattachment.

Include plastic T-fittings in the check of vacuum hoses. Check the fittings for cracks and the hose where it fits over the fitting for enlargement, which could cause leakage.

To detect vacuum leaks use a small piece of vacuum hose (1/4-inch inside diameter) as a stethoscope. Taking care not to come in contact with moving engine components, hold one end of the hose to your ear and probe around vacuum hoses and fittings, listening for the "hissing" sound characteristic of a vacuum leak.

Fuel hose

Fuel injection systems are under high pressure, even when the engine is off. Always make sure the system is depressurized before removing any hose.

Check all rubber fuel hoses for damage and deterioration. Check for cracks in areas especially where the hose bends and just before clamping points, such as where a hose attaches to the fuel injection system.

Use only high quality fuel line, specifically designed for fuel injection systems, for fuel line replacement.

Wiper blade check and replacement

Check the windshield wiper and blade assembly periodically for damage, loose components and cracked or worn blade elements. Wash the wiper blades regularly with a mild detergent solution because road film can build up and affect their efficiency.

Replace the wiper blade elements with new ones if they are cracked, worn or warped, or no longer clean adequately. It may be a good idea to replace the wiper blade and element assembly as a unit rather then just the element itself because the internal springs deteriorate over time. When buying new wiper blades, take the old ones to the auto parts store to make sure you get the right replacements.

As you remove the wiper blade, note how it is installed to simplify reinstallation.

The easiest way to remove the wiper blade is to first lift the arm assembly away from the glass for clearance (it usually locks in place). If this isn't possible, turn ignition key on and cycle the wipers to where they are accessible and turn the ignition off.

The most common type of wiper fits into a hook in the end of the wiper arm. Press on the release lever, then slide the wiper blade assembly out of the hook in the end of the arm.

After installation, make sure the components are securely mounted in the wiper frame before using the wipers.

1 Depress the release lever (finger is on it here) and slide the wiper assembly down the wiper arm and out of the hook in the end of the arm.

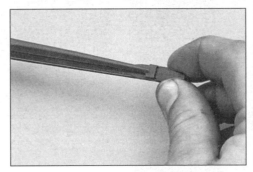

2 Squeeze the two metal prongs on the blade element to allow it to slide out of the assembly.

Tire care
Tire and tire pressure checks

Periodic inspection of the tires may spare you the inconvenience of being stranded with a flat tire. It can also provide you with vital information regarding possible problems in the steering and suspension systems before major damage occurs.

Tires are equipped with 1/2-inch wide wear bands that will appear when tread depth reaches 1/16-inch, at which point the tires can be considered worn out.

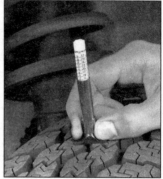

Note any abnormal tread wear. Tread pattern irregularities such as cupping, flat spots and more wear on one side than the other are indications of front end alignment and/or balance problems. If any of these conditions are noted, take the vehicle to a tire shop or service station to correct the problem.

Look closely for cuts, punctures and embedded nails or tacks. Sometimes a tire will hold air pressure for a short time or leak

Tread wear can be monitored with a simple, inexpensive device known as a tread depth indicator

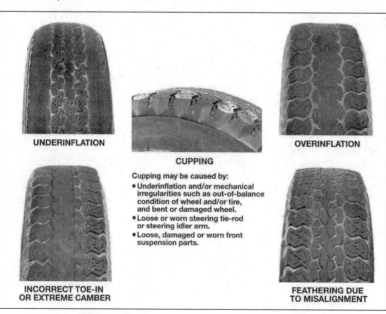

UNDERINFLATION

CUPPING

OVERINFLATION

Cupping may be caused by:
• Underinflation and/or mechanical irregularities such as out-of-balance condition of wheel and/or tire, and bent or damaged wheel.
• Loose or worn steering tie-rod or steering idler arm.
• Loose, damaged or worn front suspension parts.

INCORRECT TOE-IN
OR EXTREME CAMBER

FEATHERING DUE
TO MISALIGNMENT

This chart will help you determine the condition of the tires and the probable cause(s) of abnormal wear

If a tire loses air on a steady basis, check the valve stem core to make sure it's snug (special inexpensive wrenches are commonly available at auto parts store)

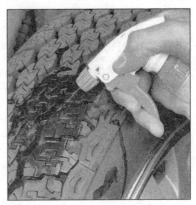

If a puncture is suspected, it can be easily verified by spraying a solution of soapy water onto the puncture area. The soapy solution will bubble if there's a leak

down very slowly after a nail has embedded itself in the tread. If a slow leak persists, check the valve stem core to make sure it's tight.

Examine the tread for an object that may have embedded itself in the tire or for a "plug" that may have begun to leak (radial tire punctures are repaired with a plug that's installed in a puncture). Unless the puncture is unusually large, a tire shop or service station can usually repair the tire.

Carefully inspect the inner sidewall of each tire for evidence of brake fluid leakage. If you see any, inspect the brakes immediately.

To extend the life of the tires, check the air pressure at least once a week with an accurate gauge (don't forget the spare)

Correct air pressure adds miles to the lifespan of the tires, improves mileage and enhances overall ride quality. Tire pressure cannot be accurately estimated by looking at a tire, especially if it's a radial. A tire pressure gauge is essential. Keep an accurate gauge in the vehicle. The pressure gauges attached to the nozzles of air hoses at gas stations are often inaccurate.

Always check tire pressure when the tires are cold. Cold, in this case, means the vehicle has not been driven over a mile in the three hours preceding a tire pressure check. A pressure rise of four to eight pounds is not uncommon once the tires are warm.

Unscrew the valve cap protruding from the wheel or hubcap and push the gauge firmly onto the valve stem. Note the reading on the gauge and compare the figure to the recommended tire pressure listed in you car's owner's manual or on the tire placard, usually located on the driver's door jamb or fuel filler door. Be sure to reinstall the valve cap to keep dirt and moisture out of the valve stem mechanism. Check all four tires and, if necessary, add enough air to bring them up to the recommended pressure.

Don't forget to keep the spare tire inflated to the specified pressure (refer to your owner's manual or the tire sidewall).

Tire rotation

The tires should be rotated every 6000 miles or six months, or whenever uneven wear is noticed.

Radial tires must be rotated in the recommended pattern. Most vehicles are equipped with *non-directional* radial tires, but some performance tires are *directional*, and have a different rotation pattern. Directional tires have an arrow on the sidewall indicating the direction they must turn when mounted on the vehicle.

Refer to the information on page 40 for the proper procedures to follow when raising the vehicle and changing a tire. Make sure the tires are blocked to prevent the vehicle from rolling as it's raised.

Preferably, the entire vehicle should be raised at the same time. This can be done on a hoist or by jacking up each corner and then lowering the vehicle onto jackstands placed under the frame rails. Always use four jackstands and make sure the vehicle is safely supported.

After rotation, check and adjust the tire pressures as necessary. Tighten the wheel lug nuts or bolts to the torque listed in your car's owner's manual.

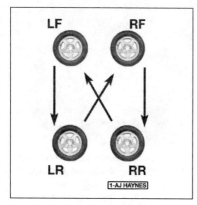

The recommended four-tire rotation pattern for *non-directional* radial tires

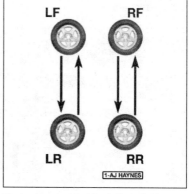

The recommended four-tire rotation pattern for *directional* radial tires

77

Battery maintenance

Note: *Some late-model vehicles will have anti-theft radios or electronic pre-sets which will be affected by disconnecting the battery. Also, the engine computer may cause the engine to run slightly rough after battery disconnection. See your owner's manual or a repair manual for additional information.*

For quick and reliable starts when you turn the key your battery has to be in top condition. To keep it that way you need to follow a routine preventive maintenance program.

Remember, before working around the battery you need proper equipment. The battery contains a dangerous fluid called electrolyte that is actually diluted sulfuric acid. Do not allow it to get in your eyes, on your skin on your clothes. Never ingest it. Keep children away from the battery. Wear protective safety glasses when working near the battery. Wear old clothes too - even diluted sulfuric acid splashed onto clothes will burn holes in them.

The battery also produces hydrogen gas, which is both flammable and explosive, so never smoke, light a match or create a spark around the battery. Before servicing the battery, always turn the engine and all accessories off and disconnect the cable from the negative terminal of the battery. Always detach the negative cable first and hook it up last when removing the battery cables!

First, check the condition of the outside of the battery. If the positive terminal and cable clamp on your vehicle's battery is equipped with a rubber protector, make sure that it's not torn or damaged. It should completely cover the terminal.

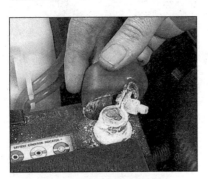

Tools and materials required for battery maintenance

Removing the cable from a battery post with a wrench - sometimes special battery pliers are required for this procedure if corrosion has caused deterioration of the nut hex (always remove the ground cable first and hook it up last!)

Battery terminal corrosion usually appears as light, fluffy powder

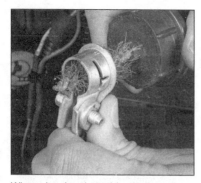

When cleaning the cable clamps, all corrosion must be removed (the inside of the clamp is tapered to match the taper on the post, so don't remove too much material)

Regardless of the type of tool used on the battery posts, a clean, shiny surface should be the result

Look for any corroded or loose connections, cracks in the case or cover or loose hold-down clamps. Next, check the entire length of each cable for cracks and frayed conductors.

Corrosion looks like white, fluffy deposits and the greatest concentrations are usually around the terminals. If you find corrosion, remove the battery for cleaning. Loosen the cable clamp bolts with a wrench, being careful to remove the ground (negative) cable first, and slide them off the terminals Then disconnect the hold-down clamp bolt and nut, remove the clamp and lift the battery from the engine compartment.

The side terminal battery brush includes a special ring-type portion used to clean the battery cable contact area of the terminal

Clean the cable clamps thoroughly with a battery brush or a terminal cleaner and a solution of warm water and baking soda. Wash the terminals and the top of the battery case with the same solution. Make sure that the solution doesn't get into the battery. Wear safety goggles and rubber gloves when cleaning the cables, terminals and battery top, to prevent any solution from coming in contact with your eyes or hands.

If the terminals have been extensively corroded, clean them up with a terminal cleaner. Thoroughly wash all cleaned areas with plain water.

Make sure that the battery tray is in good condition and the hold-down clamp bolts are tight. If the battery is removed from the tray, make sure no parts remain in the bottom of the tray when the battery is reinstalled. When reinstalling the hold-down clamp bolts, do not over-tighten them.

Corrosion on the hold-down components, battery case and surrounding areas can be removed with a solution of water and baking soda. Thoroughly rinse all cleaned areas with plain water.

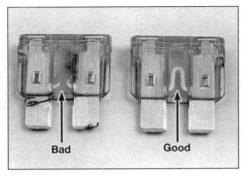

Bad   Good

When a fuse blows, the element between the terminals melts

Fuses

Fuses protect a car's electrical circuits from being overloaded. If an electrically powered item stops working, it could be that the fuse has blown. If you replace a fuse and it blows again, there's almost certainly a problem in the wiring or the item concerned. For more information on fuses and electrical systems, obtain a repair manual for your particular vehicle

How to check a fuse

The best way to check the fuses is with a test light. Check for power at the exposed terminal tips of each fuse. If power is present at one side of the fuse but not the other, the fuse is blown. A blown fuse can also be identified by visually inspecting it.

How to change a fuse

Before you start, switch off the ignition and any other electrical circuits.

WARNING

NEVER use a piece of wire, foil or any other metal in place of a fuse - not even temporarily. You will almost certainly cause damage, maybe even a fire!

1 Check your car's owner's manual for where to find the fuses. Generally, most vehicles have a fuse box under the instrument panel and another one in the engine compartment.

2 To remove a fuse, pull it straight out of the fuse box. On some cars you'll find a plastic tool for removing the fuses.

3 The new fuse must be the same amperage rating as the old one. It should be the same color, or have the same number stamped into it.

4 Push the new fuse firmly into its slot in the fuse box. Turn the ignition on and switch on the circuit concerned. If the new fuse blows, there's a problem.

Bulb replacement

Sealed-beam headlights

1 If the vehicle has retractable headlights, expose them by turning them on, then disconnect the cable from the negative terminal of the battery. Allow the headlights to cool before proceeding.

2 Remove the headlight bezel. In some cases, the bezel may be part of the vehicle's grille, so it may be necessary to remove the grille or part of the grille.

3 Remove the three or four screws that secure the headlight retainer. DON'T disturb the (usually larger) headlight adjusting screws or the adjustment will be altered. On some models with round headlights, you only need to loosen the retainer screws and rotate the retainer to disengage it from the screws.

4 Carefully remove the headlight retainer and pull the headlight out far enough to unplug the connector behind it. Remove the headlight.

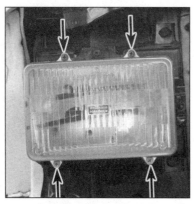

On rectangular sealed-beam headlights the retaining ring is held in place by four screws; on round headlights there are only three screws

5 Installation is the reverse of removal. Be sure the number on the lens is at the top. Check the headlights for proper operation and aiming before using them on the road. Normally, if the adjustment screws were not disturbed, the headlight will not need adjustment.

Halogen-type headlights

WARNING: These bulbs get very hot in operation. They are also gas-filled and may shatter if scratched or dropped, so wear eye protection and handle the bulbs carefully.

CAUTION: Don't touch the surface of the bulb with your fingers, because the oil from your skin could cause it to overheat and fail prematurely. If you do touch the bulb surface, clean it with rubbing alcohol.

1 Open the hood and detach the electrical connector from the headlight bulb. On some vehicles you'll have to remove a rubber cover for access to the connector.

2 On some vehicles the bulb is held in the housing with a threaded retaining ring. Remove the retaining ring by rotating it counterclockwise.

3 On some vehicles the bulb is retained by a spring clip. Squeeze the ends of the clip to disengage it from the housing.

4 Pull the bulb straight out of the socket.

5 Slide the new bulb into position. These bulbs usually have tangs around their edge so they only fit in one position. Remember, don't touch the glass surface with your fingers (if you do, clean it with rubbing alcohol). Once the tabs are aligned, push the bulb into the socket. Slip the retaining ring over the base and turn it clockwise to lock it in place, or secure it with the retaining spring, as applicable.

6 Reinstall the electrical connector and cover (if equipped) and check the lights for proper operation.

Exterior lights
Brake, turn signal, parking and back-up light bulbs

1 First, check to see if the bulb socket can be accessed from behind the lens. On rear-mounted bulbs, access is usually through the trunk (or cargo area). You may have to remove a cover to get at the bulb socket. On front-mounted bulbs, you can usually access the socket by reaching up from under the bumper. Once you've reached the bulb socket, rotate it counterclockwise about 1/4-turn and pull it out.

2 If there's no access to the bulb socket from behind the lens, there are normally screws along the outside of the lens. Remove the screws and pull the lens off. It may stick a little since there's a weather-sealing gasket behind it. If necessary, pry gently with a small screwdriver.

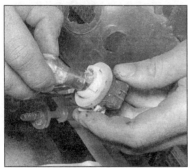

3 Bulbs with a round base like the one shown here are removed by pushing in and turn it about 1/4-turn counterclockwise. Bulbs with a flat base are removed by pulling them straight out of the socket. If the bulb is broken, remove the base of the bulb from the socket with a pair of needle-nose pliers.

4 Be sure to check the socket for corrosion, loose wires and worn or missing terminals. If the socket is corroded, clean it with a small wire brush.

5 Place the new bulb in the socket. On bulbs with a round base, align the indexing lugs with the slots in the socket, then press in firmly and rotate the bulb about 1/4-turn clockwise. On bulbs with a flat base, simply push the bulb into the socket until it seats. **Note:** *Double-filament bulbs normally have staggered indexing lugs, so, when installing the new bulb, be sure the indexing lugs match the slots in the socket.*

6 If the lens was removed, inspect the sealing gasket to be sure it's not damaged. Replace it, if necessary.

Side marker and other exterior lights

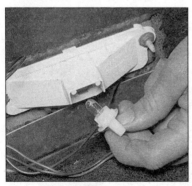

1 Much like the signal lights, side marker lights are normally accessed in one of two ways: 1) by removing the lens or 2) by removing the bulb socket from inside the trunk or cargo area (rear) or inside the fender (front).

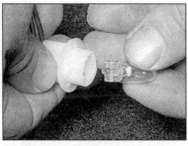

2 Press-in type side marker lights normally slide straight out of the socket, making replacement easy. Be sure to check for corrosion, loose wires and worn or missing terminals.

3 Bayonet type bulbs (bulbs with a round base) are removed by pushing in firmly and rotating the bulb 1/4-turn counterclockwise.

Engine oil and filter change

Frequent oil changes are the most important preventive maintenance procedures that can be done by the home mechanic. As engine oil ages, it becomes diluted and contaminated, which leads to premature engine wear. Generally speaking, 3000 miles or three months is a good oil change interval.

Although some sources recommend oil filter changes every other oil change, we feel that the minimal cost of an oil filter and the relative ease with which it is installed dictate that a new filter be installed every time the oil is changed.

Warm the engine to normal operating temperature (warm engine oil will drain better

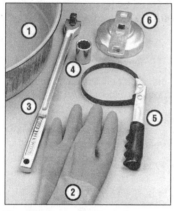

and more built-up sludge will be removed with it). If the new oil or any tools are needed, use this warm-up time to gather everything necessary for the job. The correct type of oil for your application can be found in a repair manual for your particular vehicle, available at your local auto parts store.

You should have plenty of clean rags and newspapers handy to mop up any spills. Access to the underside of the vehicle will be improved if the vehicle can be lifted on a hoist, driven onto ramps or supported by jackstands. **Warning:** *Do not work under a vehicle which is supported only by a bumper, hydraulic or scissors-type jack.*

With the engine oil warm, raise and support the vehicle. Make sure it's safely supported!

Move all necessary tools, rags and newspapers under the vehicle. Set the drain pan under the drain plug. Keep in mind that the oil will initially flow from the pan with some force; position the pan accordingly.

Use a wrench to remove the drain plug near

These tools are required when changing the engine oil and filter

1 **Drain pan** - It should be fairly shallow in depth, but wide to prevent spills

2 **Rubber gloves** - When removing the drain plug and filter, you will get oil on your hands (the gloves will prevent burns and contact with dirty engine oil)

3 **Breaker bar** - Sometimes the oil drain plug is tight, and a long breaker bar is needed to loosen it

4 **Socket** - To be used with the breaker bar or a ratchet (must be the correct size to fit the drain plug)

5 **Filter wrench** - This is a metal band-type wrench, which requires clearance around the filter to be effective

6 **Filter wrench** - This type fits on the bottom of the filter and can be turned with a ratchet or breaker bar (different-size wrenches are available for different types of filters)

Use the proper size box-end wrench or socket to remove the oil drain plug to avoid rounding it off

Since the oil filter is on very tight, you'll need a special wrench for removal - DO NOT use the wrench to tighten the new filter

Lubricate the oil filter gasket with clean engine oil before installing the filter on the engine

the bottom of the oil pan and allow the oil to drain into the pan.

After all the oil has drained, clean the drain plug and the area around the drain plug opening and reinstall the plug. Tighten the plug securely with the wrench.

Move the drain pan into position under the oil filter, then use the oil filter wrench to loosen the oil filter.

Completely unscrew the old filter. Be careful: it's full of oil. Empty the oil inside the filter into the drain pan and compare the old filter with the new one to make sure they're the same type.

Clean the area where the oil filter mounts to the engine. Check the old filter to make sure the rubber gasket isn't stuck to the engine. If the gasket is stuck to the engine, remove it.

Apply a light coat of clean oil to the rubber gasket on the new oil filter. Attach the new filter to the engine, following the tightening directions printed on the filter canister or packing box.

Lower the vehicle and locate the oil filler cap. Pour the fresh oil through the filler opening. A funnel will be helpful to avoid spills.

Add three quarts of fresh oil into the engine. Wait a few minutes, then check the level on the oil dipstick. If the oil level is above the upper mark, start the engine and allow the new oil to circulate. If the level is not up to the lower mark, add an additional quart and recheck the level. **Caution:** *Some larger engines will require a substantial amount more oil on the initial fill than this. Obtain a repair manual for your particular vehicle for the exact oil capacity.*

Run the engine for only about a minute and then shut it off. Look under the vehicle and check for leaks.

Recheck the level on the dipstick and add more oil as necessary. Add only a little at a time to prevent overfilling.

During the first few trips after an oil change, make it a point to check frequently for leaks and proper oil level.

The old oil drained from the engine cannot be reused in its present state and should be disposed of. Check with your local auto parts store, disposal facility or environmental agency to see if they will accept the oil for recycling. Don't dispose of the oil by pouring it on the ground or down a drain!

How to Wash Your Car

The first step in protecting your vehicle's appearance is to wash it regularly.

You will need:

1) A large, soft washing mitt or sponge.

2) Two buckets, one for soapy water, one for rinsing the mitt or sponge.

3) Soap designed for automotive finishes

4) Chamois, either natural or artificial: the perfect tool for drying glass and large areas of the vehicle

5) 100% cotton terrycloth towels for drying the harder-to-get-to areas and any water left after using the chamois. These towels should be washed with bleach and detergent (without liquid fabric softeners) and dried using an anti-static softener "sheet."

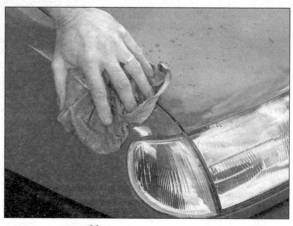

Always wash your vehicle in the shade, and cool it off first with a good rinsing before you begin to wash. Wash the body from the top down; the wheels and tires are washed last.

Put the soap in a bucket of warm water and use a strong spray of water when filling to generate lots of suds to reduce abrasion by keeping the surface "lubricated" at all times. Apply the soapy solution with the washing mitt or sponge.

Rinse the mitt or sponge frequently in the separate bucket of water. Don't put the dirty mitt or sponge back into your clean solution of soapy water. The bucket you use for rinsing the mitt or sponge should be emptied and refilled when the water gets dirty, which may be several times if the vehicle is particularly dirty.

Start with the roof and hood, then work your way down the sides, followed by front end and rear end. Do not use heavy hand pressure on your wash mitt or sponge as this will drag dirt around and scratch the paint. You can take care of stubborn spots or stains later with the proper product.

Once you have the vehicle clean, it's time to rinse it off. You must make sure to get any soapy water solution off of the finish as fast as possible. Use the hose without a nozzle for rinsing at low-pressure close to the vehicle to "flood" the body so the water comes off in sheets.

Use the chamois to clear off most of the water and the 100% cotton terrycloth towels to complete the drying.

Repairing Paint Chips and Scratches

The best way to repair chips and small scratches is to apply a small amount of exact color-matched touch-up paint.

Before you begin, find the vehicle's paint code; this will assure the correct color match. Paint codes are located in the vehicle door jamb, rear truck wall or under the hood. Refer to the Dupli-Color Color Selector Guide for additional information on locating color codes. Using the Selector Guide, look up the exact match Dupli-Color Scratch-Fix 2-in-1™ applicator that matches your color code.

Items you will need to properly repair vehicle

| Scratch-Fix 2-in-1™ applicator | Prep Wipe | Premium Touch-Up Kit |

Prepare vehicle surface first by cleaning with warm soapy water and thoroughly drying surface. Remove any wax from the area to be painted with a Dupli-Color Prep Wipe (part number PW100).

For best results, practice your repair on a smooth hard clean surface.

Spot Putty (as necessary)
Apply spot putty to deep chips or scratches using a clean straight-edge blade such as a plastic squeegee, or carefully use a razor blade. Sand putty surface smooth with enclosed sandpaper. Before sanding, allow putty to dry 30 minutes. Remove adhesive backing from sandpaper and apply to sanding block. Do not over sand.

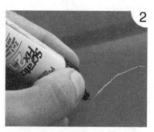

Prime Surface (as needed)
Prime bare metal with Dupli-Color Grey Primer (Part # NGSF031). Shake tube vigorously before using. Apply thin, even coats in one direction, when using roller ball or brush. Allow 10 to 20 minutes between coats. Try to contain primer application to the nick area. After use, wipe off excess primer from roller ball and replace cap. Surface will be completely dry and ready for Step 3 in 30 minutes.

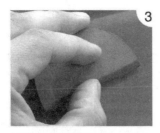

Wet Sand Primed Surface
With enclosed sandpaper and sanding block, lightly wet sand primed area until primed surface is smooth. Always keep sanding surface wet during sanding process. Do not over sand, check surface frequently (sand a few strokes and check.)

Paint – With Your Dupli-Color Exact Match Color
Apply your Dupli-Color exact match touch-up paint. Shake tube vigorously before using roller ball tip or brush. Apply a thin coat, allow 15 to 30 minutes to dry, apply second coat if necessary. After use, wipe roller ball clean and replace cap. Allow to dry thoroughly before applying Clearcoat. NOTE: If roller ball becomes clogged, hold pen upright and tap pen lightly on surface or clean roller ball tip with lacquer thinner

Clearcoat – With Dupli-Color Clear Top Coat
To ensure a perfect factory match, seal and protect your finish with the Dupli-Color Clear Top Coat provided (Part # NGSF125). Allow paint to dry 12 to 24 hours before applying Clearcoat. Shake bottle vigorously before using pen or brush applicator. To Brush: Unscrew cap and remove excess Clearcoat from brush. Apply thin coats in one direction. Cover the entire area you have repaired with a very slight overlap. (Vehicle can be used one hour after clear top coat is applied.)

Final Wet Sand
Allow Clearcoat to dry 24 hours before wet sanding. Wet sand surface with sandpaper and sanding block. Thoroughly soak paper and block before sanding. Always keep the sanding area wet during the process. Check surface smoothness frequently (sand a few strokes and check). Do not over sand. Contain sanding to the clear-coated area. Surface will haze during this process. When complete, wipe with clean dry cloth.

Final Touch – Finishing Compound
Apply Dupli-Color Finishing Compound directly to the center of the repair area. Hand buff with a clean, soft cloth. Buff straight across the repair in multiple directions. This step will remove haze, enhance color and remove light surface scratches. Re-apply to remove surface scratches if needed. (For a superior result, repeat this step after one week.) Wipe clean and apply a good car wax for maximum shine and appeal.

Working with an auto mechanic

Explaining a problem

If you've got a problem with your car, how do you explain it to the service manager or mechanic at the local repair shop? Remember that most repair shops will charge you at an hourly rate, so any extra information is likely to save you money in the long run.

If you haven't been able to identify a problem, here are a few things which you're likely to be asked when you take your car to the shop.

◆ Does the problem occur all the time, or is it intermittent?

◆ Does the problem occur when the engine's cold, hot or both?

◆ Are there any other symptoms (noises, vibration, etc)?

◆ Has the car been regularly serviced?

◆ Have you had any work done on the car recently?

If the problem occurs all the time, the best thing is to take the mechanic out for a drive and demonstrate it. If the problem is intermittent, try to take the car to the shop when the problem is present. Sometimes the shop may have no option but to replace various components until the problem disappears - this could prove to be expensive.

What's included?

The items on a bill usually fall into one of three categories: parts, labor and consumables. Always ask for an itemized list so that you can see exactly what's been included.

Whenever you're intending to get any work done, get a written estimate before you agree. It's always wise to get rough prices from several different shops so that you can compare them.

Here are a few things you should ask when getting a price for a job:

◆ What's the hourly labor rate?

◆ How long should the work take?

◆ Will new or reconditioned parts be used?

◆ Will the work be covered by a warranty? (Ask for details of the warranty)

Understanding the mechanic

When you're talking about any work to be done on your car, don't let yourself be baffled. Make sure that you understand what work the shop is intending to do. Ask if there may be any problems; for instance, there can be seized or broken fasteners to contend with, which may make the job more difficult.

Sometimes, a mechanic may point out other potential problems while carrying out work on your car. The mechanic might suggest that you'll need a set of brake discs and pads soon. Always check this for yourself, or ask to see the problem. If in doubt, ask for a second opinion from an experienced friend or another shop.

Checking the work

If components have been replaced, shops will keep the old parts handy for your inspection. It's a good idea to ask the mechanic to do this when you take your car in for work to be done.

If your car has been serviced, check that a new (clean) oil filter has been

installed, and pull out the dip-stick to check for fresh oil. You should be able to tell where work has been done, because the area around the work should be cleaner than the rest of the car.

If the work involved disturbing any gaskets or seals, park the car overnight with a sheet of cardboard or paper underneath (or pick a clean piece of road or driveway) so that you can check for signs of leaks in the morning. If you notice any leaks, take the car back to have them fixed, and don't let the shop charge you for fixing the problem (unless it's totally unrelated to the work they've done).

Checking the bill

Always ask for an itemized bill, which will give you a full breakdown of all the costs, and will allow you to see exactly what work has been done.

◆ Check the details of the bill against the estimate, and ask about any discrepancies. If you find that "miscellaneous" costs appear on your bill, ask what they are.

◆ Check the labor costs against the shop's quoted hourly rate, and check the price of any parts used (see "What's included?").

◆ Check that the work described on the bill has been carried out (see "Checking the work"), and if there's any evidence that you've been billed for work which hasn't been done, ask the mechanic.

Warning lights

Your car has various warning lights to warn you of problems with your car's systems. Some warnings are more serious than others, so here's a guide as to what the more common warning lights mean, and what to do if they come on. For more information on these faults and how to correct them, purchase a repair manual for your particular vehicle from your local auto parts store.

Warning light	What does it mean?	What should I do?
Brake fluid level warning* or **BRAKE**	Low brake fluid level	• Don't drive the car • Check brake fluid level and top up if necessary • Check for brake fluid leaks. If you find a leak, don't drive until the leak has been fixed
Parking brake "on" warning*	Parking brake is applied	• Check that parking brake is fully released
Charge warning	Alternator is not fully charging the battery	• The car can be driven, but don't drive too far or your battery may go dead • Have the alternator and its wiring checked as soon as possible
Oil pressure warning	Engine oil pressure low	• Stop the engine immediately, check the oil level and look for oil leaks, then call for assistance if necessary. Serious damage could be caused if you run the engine
Coolant temperature warning	Coolant temperature excessive	• Stop as soon as possible. Allow the engine to cool completely, then check the coolant level; add if necessary. • If the light comes on again within a short distance, stop and call for assistance
Engine system warning CHECK or	Trouble code stored in engine management self-diagnostic system	• The car can be driven, but you may notice a loss of performance. Have the engine management system checked as soon as possible

Warning light	What does it mean?	What should I do?
ABS warning (ABS or ((ABS)))	ABS malfunction	• The car can be driven, but the ABS may not be working (normal braking will not be affected). Have the ABS tested as soon as possible
Airbag (or SRS) warning	Airbag system problem	• The car can be driven, but the airbag system may not work in the event of an accident. Have the airbag system checked as soon as possible
Low fuel warning	Low fuel level in tank	• Fill up soon!

*Note: *Sometimes two or more of the brake warning lights are combined. If you suspect that the light may indicate low brake fluid level, DO NOT drive the car until you've checked the level, added if necessary, and checked for leaks.*

meijer COUPON

$5 OFF
with coupon

ANY AUTOMOTIVE BATTERY

Automotive Dept.

meijer

COUPON GOOD THRU 7/3/05
Present to cashier prior to making your purchase
LIMIT ONE ITEM AND COUPON PER FAMILY

5 41250 33834 0

---

meijer COUPON

$5 OFF
with coupon

VEC-1088A BATTERY CHARGER OR VEC-022 JUMPSTARTER

Automotive Dept.

meijer

COUPON GOOD THRU 7/3/05
Present to cashier prior to making your purchase
LIMIT ONE ITEM AND COUPON PER FAMILY

5 41250 33835 7

---

meijer COUPON

$5 OFF
with coupon

SPORTS CHARGER
No.SE2151MA.

Automotive Dept.

meijer

COUPON GOOD THRU 7/3/05
Present to cashier prior to making your purchase
LIMIT ONE ITEM AND COUPON PER FAMILY

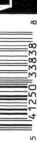

5 41250 33838 8

keep it charged

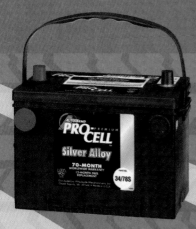

$5 OFF

with coupon

Any One Automotive Battery

$5 OFF

with coupon

VEC-1088A Battery Charger or VEC-022 Jumpstarter

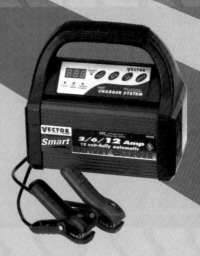

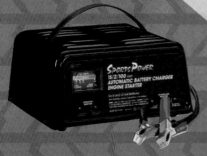

$5 OFF

with coupon

Sports Charger No.SE2151MA.

meijer COUPON

BUY FIVE, GET ONE
FREE
with coupon

QUART CASTROL
SYNTEC OIL

Automotive Dept.

meijer COUPON GOOD THRU 7/3/05
Present to cashier prior to making your purchase
LIMIT ONE ITEM AND COUPON PER FAMILY

---

meijer COUPON

$5 OFF
with coupon

ANY CASE OF
CASTROL
SYNTEC OIL

Automotive Dept.

meijer COUPON GOOD THRU 7/3/05
Present to cashier prior to making your purchase
LIMIT ONE ITEM AND COUPON PER FAMILY

---

meijer COUPON

$3 OFF

ANY AIR FILTER
With coupon and purchase of
any two (2) oil filters.

Automotive Dept.

meijer COUPON GOOD THRU 7/3/05
Present to cashier prior to making your purchase
LIMIT ONE ITEM AND COUPON PER FAMILY

keep it running smooth

BUY FIVE, GET ONE FREE

with coupon

Quart Castrol Syntec Oil

$5 OFF

with coupon

Any Case of Castrol Syntec Oil

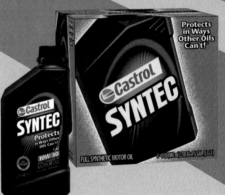

$3 OFF

Any Air Filter

with coupon and purchase of any two Oil Filters

meijer COUPON

$5 OFF
with coupon

ULTIMATE SAFETY KIT

Automotive Dept.

meijer

COUPON GOOD THRU 7/3/05
Present to cashier prior to making your purchase
LIMIT ONE ITEM AND COUPON PER FAMILY

---

meijer COUPON

BUY ONE, GET ONE
FREE
with coupon

FIX A FLAT WITH HOSE
16 oz. No.S-420.

Automotive Dept.

meijer

COUPON GOOD THRU 7/3/05
Present to cashier prior to making your purchase
LIMIT ONE ITEM AND COUPON PER FAMILY

---

meijer COUPON

$5 OFF
with coupon

TRICO TEFLON BLADES
Excludes winter blades.

Automotive Dept.

meijer

COUPON GOOD THRU 7/3/05
Present to cashier prior to making your purchase
LIMIT ONE ITEM AND COUPON PER FAMILY